simply
enough!

JESUS
PLUS
NOTHING

TIM TIMMONS

Copyright © 2013 by Tim Timmons

Published by Embers Press, 2618 San Miguel Dr., Newport Beach, CA 92660.

ADVANCING THE CONVERSATION OF JESUS

eBook at www.timtimmons.com

Audio at www.timtimmons.com

Library of Congress Control Number: 2013937802

Scripture quotations marked (MSG) are taken from *The Message.* Copyright © 1993, 1994, 1995, 1996, 2000, 2001, 2002. Used by permission of NavPress Publishing Group. Scripture quotations marked (NASB) are taken from the NEW AMERICAN STANDARD BIBLE®, Copyright © 1960, 1962, 1963, 1968, 1971, 1972, 1973, 1975, 1977, 1995 by The Lockman Foundation. Used by permission. Scripture quotations marked (NIV) are taken from THE HOLY BIBLE, NEW INTERNATIONAL VERSION®, NIV®. Copyright © 1973, 1978, 1984, 2011 by Biblica, Inc.™ Used by permission. All rights reserved worldwide. Scripture quotations marked (NIV1984) are taken from the HOLY BIBLE, NEW INTERNATIONAL VERSION®. Copyright © 1973, 1978, 1984 by Biblica. Used by permission of Zondervan. All rights reserved. Scripture quotations marked (PHILLIPS) are taken from J. B. Phillips, *The New Testament in Modern English,* 1962 edition, published by HarperCollins. Scripture quotations marked (TNIV) are taken from the HOLY BIBLE, TODAY'S NEW INTERNATIONAL VERSION®, TNIV®, Copyright © 2001, 2005 by Biblica®. All rights reserved worldwide.

ISBN: 978-0-98424-299-3 (trade paper)

Cover and interior design: Mark & Kim Seigler

Printed in the United States of America

15 16 17 18 19 SBI 9 8 7 6 5 4 3 2

I am afraid that, as the serpent deceived

Eve by his craftiness, your minds

will be led astray from the simplicity

and purity of devotion to Christ.

—

The apostle Paul (2 Corinthians 11:3 NASB)

Contents

Prologue: What If . . . ?

What if Jesus alone is really all we need? What if Jesus is the gospel and not the many things we make it?

Could it be that Jesus wasn't a Christian, wasn't the founder of Christianity, and isn't owned by Christianity?

Is it possible, in fact, that the organized Church was never Jesus' intention? That he's really more interested in the Kingdom? Interestingly, Jesus only mentions the church on two occasions.

Despite all the attention given to large and growing Churches, what if there's more spiritual power when a few are gathered in Jesus' name than when masses flock to Church?

How could Jesus' simple invitation "Follow me" be his most revolutionary words?

What if God has planted seeds in all the world's cultures to prepare people for recognizing Jesus as someone special?

What if Jesus never commanded us to convert people to a religious system?

———————

Is it true that God is calling people from every culture around the world to himself? Is there any chance that it might be possible to be a genuine follower of Jesus and still be a Muslim, Hindu, Buddhist, animist, or agnostic? Is it possible that Jesus is the name above all names and not limited to any socio-religious community—not even yours?

———————

Imagine if there's a movement underway that's invisible to most people and yet huge, widespread, and unstoppable—and just what Jesus wants to happen in the world today.

———————

My take on these issues has changed dramatically from what it once was. Don't get me wrong: I loved the Church then and I love the Church now. I have no intent to bash the Church. I'm not dismissing the Church. What I am saying is that it seems clear that Jesus viewed the "church" as followers gathering in his name, participating and interacting with one another, not as a group of spectators.

In *Simply Enough* I'll tell you something of my own journey. I'll also open Scripture to reveal some insights you may never have seen there before. And finally I'll connect it all with what's happening today when Jesus shows up in my own culture and in every culture around the world. I promise you it's so much greater than Church as most of us think about it.

Whatever you think about Jesus . . .

Whatever your views about Christianity . . .

Whatever your religious background . . .

. . . there's something big happening today, and it's all about Jesus. I don't want to miss being a part of it. I don't think you will either. And the thing is, it starts so *simply!*

CHAPTER 1

Jesus vs. Religion

Hi, I'm Tim Timmons and I'm an addict.

A religion addict.

Of all the addictions, none other is so insidious as religion. No drug hooks its victim like this one. No form of alcohol offers such a high. And no other addiction is so hard to break.

Compounding the problem, the religious addiction is legal. No one is going to take away your keys to the Kingdom if you're a religion addict. No one is going to stage an intervention. No one is going to tell you to cut back, to get help, to give it up.

Just the opposite. You are going to be everyone's go-to guy or girl when something needs to be done in your Church or religious organization. You're going to be the one they ask to head the committee. You're going to be the one they want on point, because you're the person who can get it done and get it done right.

Let's face it, something about that is intoxicating. It feels good to be needed. To be wanted. To be depended upon like that. It makes shots at the bar seem like light beer by comparison.

But here's the thing about the highs of addiction. They don't last. And after the high, there's the hangover. Or the withdrawal. So, to get over that pain, we go back for more of what made us high in the first place.

Let me be clear. I am not just talking about an individual addiction to religion, which was my kind of addiction and maybe is yours. I'm also talking about a whole culture that is in the throes of addiction. Our Christian culture has been on a bender so long that it can't see itself the way other people at the party see it. And it's not a pretty picture. Trust me, I've heard the hushed conversations while we're in the room, along with the harsh criticisms when we've left.

To be honest, after looking at my past self in the mirror, I think the revulsion is justified.

My History as a Christian

As an only child, I was driven to perform. My parents expected me to excel, and I did my best to live up to their expectations. I was the first on either side of the family to go to college. It was a Christian liberal arts college, where I was a favorite among my professors and a leader among my peers. After college, I went to Dallas Theological Seminary, which was the best, according to those same professors and peers.

At seminary, again, I performed well. And when I graduated, I left that academic nest on the updrafts of everyone's highest hopes. By then, I had degrees, acclaim, an extensive library of books on fixing people, and a waiting list of people who needed to be fixed.

I put out my shingle: "Tim Timmons. Equipped for Ministry." And I started my practice. I had such a great start, or so it seemed to me then. The best theological training. Plenty of gifting. And a passion to change the world, one person at a time, one book at a time, one crowd at a time.

I lacked only one thing.

Jesus.

At best, I viewed his statements in the Gospels as proof texts to be used in evangelistic discussions and debates. But I didn't love him. At least not the way he was loved by those who first knew him, first followed him.

What I loved was performing. And over time I got pretty good at it, leading a large Church, writing books, getting known. It made my family proud, my college proud, my seminary proud. And that felt good. *Really* good.

But I craved more: one more exhilarating counseling appointment, where I turned someone's life around; one more dynamic speaking engagement, where I wowed the crowd; one more best seller, where I . . .

. . . could get high again.

After years of living like this, everything started to crumble. My marriage, my family. I was exhausted—physically, emotionally, and spiritually. I was frustrated and disillusioned. I felt like a fraud.

How did I lose my way? I cried out from the throes of withdrawal. *And how—if ever—can I find my way to enough?*

But remember, I said the whole Christian culture has a similar addiction problem. It turns out, Christianity has a past with a contour similar to my own.

The History of Christianity

For the first three hundred years of its existence, Christianity was a despised religion and Christians were a persecuted minority. But then in AD 315 the emperor Constantine signed an imperial edict, not only ending three centuries of state-sponsored persecution but also making Christianity the official state religion. The state had finally embraced the Church. And the Church had returned the embrace. At best, it was an unequal yoking; at worst, an unholy union.

Almost immediately, Christians began destroying pagan temples, along with their priests. In 356, attending pagan services became punishable by death. In the fifth century, the Christian emperor Theodosius went so far as to have children executed for playing with fragments of pagan statues. By the sixth century, pagans were stripped of their rights.

But it wasn't enough.

During the eighth century, Charlemagne waged war against those whom the Roman Empire had determined were heathens. His battle cry was "Saxony must be Christianized or wiped out." He proceeded to do just that. During his reign, most of Europe's indigenous cultures were obliterated.

The height of atrocities during this period took place in 782 when Charlemagne captured a large crowd of Saxons in battle. He herded them to a river and there gave them the choice—be baptized in the name of the Lord Jesus Christ or be beheaded. Over four thousand lost their heads that day.

By the year 800, Charlemagne was crowned emperor by Pope Leo III. In 1165 he was canonized as a saint. All this for the ruthless and relentless war he waged.

But it wasn't enough.

On the command of Pope Urban II in 1095, the Crusades began. Jerusalem was conquered four years later, leaving over sixty thousand men, women, and children slaughtered in the streets. The archbishop of

Tyre, who witnessed the slaughter, wrote:

> It was impossible to look upon the vast numbers of the slain
> without horror; everywhere lay fragments of human bodies,
> and the very ground was covered with the blood of the slain.
> It was not only the spectacle of headless bodies and mutilated
> limbs strewn in all directions that roused the horror of all who
> looked upon them. Still more dreadful was it to gaze upon the
> victors themselves, dripping with blood from head to foot, an
> ominous sight, which brought terror to all who met them. It
> is reported that within the Temple enclosure alone about ten
> thousand infidels perished.

Figures vary, but by the end of the Crusades, Christians had killed between twenty million and sixty million people.

Got that? *Between twenty million and sixty million.*

Each victim of fanatical Christianity was made in the image of God. Each had a name. Along with each name went a story. And each story was cut short with a sword or a spear or some unspeakably gruesome means of torture.

The blood of Christian conquest stained the pages of history, seeping through the centuries and spreading across continents.

Take Columbus, for example. Here is the part of his story you probably didn't learn in school.

Columbus wrote in his logbook why he set sail across the Atlantic: "to bring the Gospel of Jesus Christ to the heathens." Though he found the people of the New World loving and generous, beginning with his second voyage his men looted their villages, killed their animals, and slaughtered or enslaved the villagers. Columbus' son Fernando chronicled the atrocities. If the natives resisted, Columbus countered their resistance by saying, "With the help of God . . . we shall make war against you in all ways and manners that we can, and shall subject you to the yoke of obedience to the Church and of their highnesses. We shall take you and your wives and your children, and shall make slaves of them."[1]

But making slaves of them wasn't enough. On that second voyage Spanish soldiers invented all manner of gruesome ways to purge the land of these "infidels." They built low gallows, where the toes of those who hung on them barely touched the ground. The gallows had room for thirteen natives—the number was chosen in "honor" of Christ and his twelve disciples. And while they dangled the victims, the Spaniards wrapped straw around their bodies and burned them.

I'm not exaggerating to make a point. These things really happened. They happened "in the name of our Lord Jesus Christ."

And—God help us—they are happening still.

We have beaten our swords into words and our spears into sound bites. With them we wage war. Instead of actual wars, they are cultural wars. We do this because we believe we have cornered the market on truth. Not only do we believe we have cornered the market; we believe we have the concession rights to that corner. The result has been the marketing of Christianity. And so the marketing mantra of the twenty-first-century Church has become "Bigger, better, faster!"

More. More. More.

As if "mega" wasn't enough. How did the Church lose its way? And how—if ever—can it find the way to enough?

His Story

The story of Jesus is a different story. It chronicles a way of peace, not war; a way of love, not hate; a way of compassion, not cruelty. When Jesus taught his followers to love their enemies, he illustrated that teaching with his life. On the night Jesus was taken captive, Peter pulled a sword and cut off the ear of one of his captors. Jesus not only told his follower to put away the sword; he picked up the severed ear and put it back on the wounded man's head, healing him.[2]

The only blood Jesus allowed to be shed "in his name" was his own.

That is who he was, who he is, and who he will always be. He is the Lamb of God, not a wolf in sheep's clothing; the Prince of Peace, not a potentate of politics; the Wonderful Counselor, not a bloodthirsty crusader.

That is *his* story.

In the three centuries after Jesus, poles with his impaled followers on them lined Roman roads. Those who followed him, followed him to death. They were humiliated, persecuted, tortured, and put on display in the most gruesome of ways in public arenas to the cheers of Roman audiences thirsting for blood.

When Christianity became the state-sponsored religion of the Roman Empire, you might think those Christians would have kept following Jesus down the path he had blazed for them—loving their enemies, praying for those who persecuted them, blessing those who cursed them. But instead of turning the other cheek, they took to the streets. They tore down pagan temples, killed their priests, and purged the land of infidels. The persecuted became the persecutors.

How, for the love of God, did it happen?

It happened the same way it happens today.

It happens when we don't believe that Jesus alone is enough. It happens when we believe that we have to have political influence, more seats in Congress, more votes. It happens when we believe we have to have money—the more the better—in order to advance the Kingdom of God. It happens when we believe we have to have power in every sphere of influence from the city council to the US Supreme Court. It happens when we believe that we have to get more people and more buildings so those people can come together. And *better* buildings so we can attract *better* people—richer people, more influential people. After all, to do more we have to have more.

This has been the math that Christianity has used over the centuries. The formula is: Jesus + something = more than Jesus alone.

I lived that formula most of my life. Until I did the math.

I urge you to do the math too.

Jesus plus something doesn't increase him; it diminishes him. It isn't more; it is less. Because implicit in the plus sign is that Jesus alone isn't enough. Isn't simply enough.

Your Story

What is *your* history? And how did it begin? Who did you follow, and why? (Or maybe the question should be, *what* did you follow, and why?) Where has that road taken you and how do you feel about where you are now?

In the Upper Room, shortly before Jesus was captured, interrogated, and tortured to death, one of his followers asked where he was going. Show us the way, he said, so we can follow you.[3]

Jesus responded by saying, "I am the way."[4]

He didn't say a religion was the way. Or a certain sect within that religion. He didn't say a creed was the way. Or a set of spiritual exercises. He said he was the way.

As Jesus walked the fragrant shores of Galilee, people came and saw, came and listened, came and followed. There were no conditions to follow him. No doctrinal statement you had to sign off on. No pledge you had to commit to. You weren't flagged for your ethnicity or refused for your morality. Your sex didn't qualify you or disqualify you; neither did your standing in the community. His appeal was simple:

> Are you tired? Worn out? Burned out on religion? Come to me. Get away with me and you'll recover your life. I'll show you how to take a real rest. Walk with me and work with me—watch how I do it. Learn the unforced rhythms of grace. I won't lay anything heavy or ill-fitting on you. Keep company with me and you'll learn to live freely and lightly.[5]

To those hunched over their nets or their accounting tables, to those who were worn out and burned out on religion, Jesus said, "Come."

To those of us today who are hunched over our desks or our computer tables, to those of us who are worn out and burned out, he still says, "Come."

He doesn't say, "Come to Christianity." He doesn't say, "Come to Church." He says, "Come to *me.*"

What he offers when we come is recovery. Recovery of the life we have lost along the way, the rhythms we have lost along the way, the freedom and the lightness we have lost along the way. He calls us not to a guilt trip but to a getaway.

This is *his* way, a way largely without words and certainly without swords.

When I came off withdrawal from my addiction to religion, I looked at this Jesus, this one who for so long had been unknown to me. And I listened to him, this one to whom I had turned a deaf ear for so long.

"Come to me," he said, smiling. And I came.

As I followed him, I came to know him. As I came to know him, I came to love him. In loving him, I realized he was enough, realized I was enough. Just as I am. Without one plea. And without one performance.

It is *this* Jesus I want you to come and see, the one I have followed along the shores of the past several years, and from whom I have learned the unforced rhythms of grace.

He was my rest and my recovery.

Perhaps he will be yours.

Unforced rhythms of grace.

CHAPTER 2

No Substitutions

Is Jesus simply enough?

Take all the time you need to answer that question to your own satisfaction. A lot is at stake.

As you consider the question, let me share some thoughts throughout the rest of this book that I hope will be helpful. For it's a question we all have to answer. But I can't answer it for you, and you can't answer it for me.

Each of us has to answer it not with a word, or with a signature, or with a vote. We have to answer it with our lives.

It is perhaps the only question that matters, for the answer will determine not only the course of your life but also the quality of your life.

Pure and Simple

Jesus made it clear that he was enough. His revolutionary call has always been "Follow me!" The call is not to follow a religious system or a set of rules, whether it's his or anybody else's. The call is:

"Follow *me!*"

It's not about following propaganda. It's not about following a program. It's about following a person. This is what sets Jesus apart from all other great leaders. He stands out by embodying his teachings. Truth is not a principle or a proposition or a set of beliefs. It is a person who calls all of us into relationship with him.

Jesus didn't just *teach* the truth; he *is* the truth. He doesn't call us to simply know *things*, but to know *him*. He teaches us to be *with him*. Not to walk in lockstep with everything he said, without doubts or questions or confusion. But to walk alongside him, to watch and to learn. To keep company with him, to rest and recover. To walk in rhythm with him—a graceful rhythm, not a forceful one. He doesn't weigh us down with the law. He lightens our load with his love. And step by step with him, day by day with him, we will learn to live freely and lightly.

Jesus' first step in introducing this new lifestyle was to gather a small circle of men. His purpose wasn't to form a focus group to clarify his message. It wasn't to form a strategic planning committee to figure out the best way to get that message to the masses. Rather, it was to gather a few followers around him, simply to be with him.[6] Just him.

Apparently Jesus thought that he alone was enough.

Within that circle of twelve close friends, three—Peter, James, and John—were the closest to Jesus. When Jesus took those three up on the mountain to pray, he was fully revealed to them, transfigured into a bright flash of lightning from head to toe. At this amazing moment, Moses and Elijah appeared in glorious splendor, talking with Jesus. When the three disciples saw this, Peter wanted to put up three shelters—one for Jesus, one for Moses, and one for Elijah. The instant he suggested it, a cloud appeared, covering them with glory and filling them with fear. A voice came from the cloud, saying, "This is my Son, whom I have chosen; listen to him." When the voice had spoken, they found that Jesus was alone. Moses the lawgiver and Elijah the prophet had vanished, and all that was left was Jesus, simply and solely Jesus. [7]

Apparently the Father felt that Jesus alone was enough.

Now let's look at someone much more like us—Peter.

After the resurrection of Jesus, his disciples were despondent and went back to fishing in the Sea of Galilee. Peter was especially feeling a sense of guilt because of his repeated denials of Jesus back in Jerusalem. What must have been most hurtful was that Jesus had warned him of his defection in advance. At that time Peter's response was to declare his allegiance, vowing never to do such a thing.[8] But when he was identified that night by a small crowd around a campfire, he sweated from the fear of being handed over to the authorities, and he buckled under the pressure.[9]

That would seem to be the end of Peter's story as a follower of Jesus. And it would have been if he had been a pastor of a contemporary Church or a leader of a religious organization. You would think his failure as a follower would have been grounds for dismissal. You would think his defection would have disqualified him. But notice how Jesus handled the situation.

Peter, along with several other defectors, fled to the Sea of Galilee, hoping to find solace in the familiar lapping of the waves or at least distraction from the pain by going fishing. That is just where Jesus showed up, not in the synagogue but on the shore, where *they* were. And he made them *breakfast*. Can you imagine what Peter was thinking? His guilt level must have been high, expecting Jesus to confront him with "I told you so, Peter." But Jesus didn't do that.

As they ate breakfast together, all were quiet. I'm sure they were fearful of what Jesus might have been thinking and what he was going to say. After they finished the meal, Jesus turned to Peter. What will he say? they must have wondered. And none more so than Peter himself.

Here's what he said: "Peter, do you love me?"[10]

What a shock those words must have been! Peter was perhaps expecting a lecture on how he had failed at his duty. Failed as a follower. Failed as a friend. But Jesus didn't talk to him about duty. Rather, he talked to him about devotion. Jesus had only one concern, and it was not about responsibility but relationship. He wanted to know Peter's heart and where it stood in relation to him. Jesus wanted to give Peter a chance to declare his relationship with him, openly and without fear. A second chance. And as if that weren't shocking enough, Jesus repeated the question, giving Peter another opportunity to publicly declare his devotion.

"Do you love me?"

"Do you love me?"

Jesus was trying to make a point with his most devoted followers. And the point is this: he was not concerned with their screw-ups or their shortcomings; he was only concerned with their relationship with him.

Jesus is trying to make the same point with you and with me. Our relationship with him is enough, he's saying. I am safe, warm, and welcoming, no matter what you've done or haven't done. You can come to me without fear.

I am enough, he was saying then to his followers. Apparently they got it.

I am enough, he is saying now to you and to me.

It's that simple.

That pure and that simple.

Will we get it?

How We Miss It

If Jesus presented himself as enough, and if those he touched believed he was enough, why do we miss this point, which is the very essence of the good news of Jesus?

We are able to develop entire belief systems around Jesus, enlist the masses to join our organizations around Jesus, judge those who do not see eye to eye with us about Jesus, and propagate these belief systems, organizations, and dogma as the only way to life—yet all without getting to know this Jesus personally.

How is it that we can miss the truth that Jesus is enough?

There are at least three subtle ways this occurs.

First, we have a tendency to add something unnecessary to Jesus. This "something" takes the form of man-made commandments and long-standing traditions. In other words, it's Jesus with additives.[11]

I understand this tendency, because I share in it. I'm often tempted to help Jesus out—to work for him in an advisory capacity. I seem to drift into thinking that my ideas and visions are better than his. Otherwise, I would ask Jesus more often what he has in mind.

One of the most common ways I've found to add something unnecessary is to think that *what* you know is more important than *who* you know. This leads most Church leaders to put an overemphasis upon programs and classes, believing that the impartation of information—transferring techniques and a set of beliefs—is vital to the spiritual life. As one of my pastor friends says, "It's creating a YMCA organization for God!"

I used to pride myself in how many people I had enrolled in discipleship classes. At one point we were "discipling" over a thousand believers in a series of four classes. We called it Christianity 101, and we were quite impressed with ourselves.

I am aware of a large Church that places so much emphasis upon the "How many?" question in each department that this has become the primary reason for hiring and firing staff.

The raw truth is that, when the many are gathered, it's the most ineffective method of making disciples. Yet this is held up as the best method—the more, the merrier!

Second, we have a tendency to hold as sacred something that has become a substitute for Jesus. These substitutes can be your sacred scriptures, your revered saints, your religious services, your particular organization or denomination, your cultural identification or religious icons.

Today, in particular, we hold on to our favorite doctrines or teachings, no matter what Jesus says about it! This is just what Jesus warned the religious leadership about. He pointed out to them that they were diligent in searching the Scriptures, believing that in those Scriptures is eternal life. Then he clarified his point by saying, "These are the very Scriptures that testify about me, yet you refuse to come to me to have life."[12]

This same tendency is alive and well today. Many of us have become worshipers of the Scriptures as the substitute for Jesus—the giver of eternal life. This is called *bibliolatry*, which is the worship of the Bible, or more accurately, the worship of your own or someone else's interpretation of the Bible.

In the Christian world, this may be the most sensitive topic of discussion of all. It seems difficult to enter into a personal relationship with

Jesus day in and day out. It's much easier to measure your life against a system of dos and don'ts. It's easier because it's all contained within your spiritual box. To enter into a dynamic relationship with the Person of Jesus is not so easy; it's difficult and messy! This is why I say that following and walking with Jesus is the most difficult thing I've ever attempted to do.

Third, we have a tendency to leave Jesus behind. Whether it is in newsletters, religious services, sermons, articles, prayers, or worship experiences, Jesus is embarrassingly left behind. Even where two are three are gathered together in his name, he is often left out of our conversations.

I have a new hobby. I make it a habit to look for Jesus everywhere I go. I look for Jesus in a Church service and have been dumbfounded to sit through an entire service and never hear the name of Jesus. I read Christian newsletters and websites and am amazed to read about everything else while Jesus is being left out. I read in a major magazine an interview of a fellow pastor who has become huge in the marketplace. He was sharing his plan to change the world. However, to my great discouragement, Jesus didn't even get honorable mention.

You must understand how I have become so good at noticing when Jesus is left out. The true source of my being dumbfounded, amazed, and discouraged is that these are the things I did when I was "hot" and sought after in the Christian marketplace. I continually left Jesus out. And what's worse is that today I am still capable of leaving Jesus behind or leaving Jesus out of my actions altogether! The only reason for any degree of success in keeping Jesus primary in my thinking and communication comes from hanging out with other followers who are struggling with the same things.

These tendencies take away from the message of Jesus. They diminish Jesus by adding something unnecessary to him, by replacing him with something, and by leaving him and his message behind. These tendencies amount to a deadly triad that keeps us from seeing Jesus clearly.

If we can't see him, how will we ever be able to know him? And if we can't know him, how will we ever be able to know if he is enough?

Is Jesus Simply Enough?

Back to my original question. It's not one I am pressing you to answer. It's one I'm simply asking you to consider. You've begun to take a look at Jesus, what he said, what he did. You've begun to take a look at what others thought about him, said about him. You've come and you've seen. Where are you in your thinking?

I've adapted the conclusion to this chapter from part of Chip Brogden's essay "Is Jesus Enough?"[13] Read through it slowly, reflecting on the state of things in your religious circle and the state of things in your own soul.

When apostles love Church planting and mission work more than Jesus, they are saying that Jesus is not enough.

When prophets love their prophecies, dreams, and visions more than they love Jesus, they are saying that Jesus is not enough.

When evangelists love traveling, preaching, and going to meetings more than they love Jesus, they are saying that Jesus is not enough.

When pastors love Church services and building programs more than they love Jesus, they are saying that Jesus is *who says any of these people love anything more than Jesus?*

not enough.

When teachers love their teachings more than they love Jesus, they are saying that Jesus is not enough.

When preachers love their preaching more than they love Jesus, they are saying that Jesus is not enough.

When ministers love their ministry more than they love Jesus, they are saying that Jesus is not enough.

When musicians love their music more than they love Jesus, they are saying that Jesus is not enough.

When writers love their writings more than they love Jesus, they are saying that Jesus is not enough.

When any of us grow tired of "just" being with Jesus, longing for something bigger, something better, something greater, something more powerful, something other than what we have in Jesus already, we are saying that Jesus is not enough.

How about you? If Jesus were all *you* had, would he be enough?

Please note that when I speak of Jesus being enough, I am not talking religiously or in some otherworldly sense. I don't believe Jesus is "out there" somewhere. Just as Jesus taught about his Kingdom, his presence is near—here among us all.[14] Jesus is personally and readily available to anyone who is willing to seek him out.

We live in a world where people are looking for something tangible and authentic, for someone to care and someone who can offer real solutions to their questions and struggles. Later in this book you will be able to see clearly from the mouth of Jesus what he is able to do for anyone who will come and seek him out. Jesus can personally be the dynamic and real answer to your fears, your anger issues, your guilt, the shame that has nearly drowned you, or whatever is working in your soul.

CHAPTER 3

Backed into a Corner

When I graduated from Dallas Theological Seminary, I was launched into the world with diploma in hand, principles in tow, answers in mind, and an air of arrogance that is captured in this persistent saying: "You can always tell a Dallas man . . . but you can't tell him much!"

I was successful right out of the chute. But as I said in chapter 1, it wasn't enough. It was never enough. And so I just kept adding more onto my schedule, onto my list of responsibilities, onto my accomplishments. Over time, though, the burden of more weighed me down, let me down, and finally brought me down.

That's when I met Jesus. He was different from what I expected. He was different from the Christian faculty who educated me, different from the Christian crowds who flocked around me, different from the Christian friends who deserted me.

Jesus was the one who stayed. He was the one who didn't shake his head in disappointment, didn't turn away in disgust. He was the one who knelt down, picked me up, dusted me off. He is the one who embraced me. It was then that I realized the Jesus I had first embraced was different from the one who was embracing me now.

And I realized something else.

This Jesus I could follow.

This Jesus I wanted to follow, needed to follow, couldn't help but follow.

Not the Jesus who is wrapped up in a religious system of dos and don'ts. Not the Jesus who is used to raise money to build more and more buildings and fill the religious treasuries. Not the Jesus who was hijacked for the violent Crusades. Not the Jesus who is embraced by a political candidate or party to impress the people. Not the Jesus who wants you to join his club. Not the Jesus who lays a guilt trip on you for not performing. Not the hellfire and damnation Jesus, nor the meek and mild Jesus.

This Jesus is the one I never really knew. The one without Christian verbiage. The one without religious baggage. The one without self-righteous garbage.

This Jesus is simply enough.

I no longer have any desire to back someone into a boxlike way of thinking about Jesus. Why should I limit who can follow Jesus or even relate to him? If you must believe Jesus is this or is that before you can relate to him, then you may have no option to get to know him as the disciples did.

A Diversity of Followers

The Jesus I met is the Jesus that the early followers, called disciples, got to know. For three and a half years they were in an apprentice relationship with Jesus. In their system of education, they never made the grade of being chosen by a rabbi to follow in his steps, so they had returned home to work the family business. But this rabbi, this Jesus, this new guy in town, chose them to follow him. He picked untrained, ordinary men to come along with him and learn from him. In a sense, Jesus chose those who hadn't made the cut, walk-ons, as the team he wanted on the field in the most important game in the history of the world.

From those early beginnings, the Jesus movement continues to be the largest in the world today. This all-encompassing movement includes people from every culture and religion on the earth—Christians, Muslims, Buddhists, Jews, Hindus, Sikhs, pantheists, agnostics. When Jesus is not boxed into any religious system or wrapped up in a package marked "Exclusive," he becomes universally attractive throughout the world. People from every culture embrace Jesus, simply Jesus, whether they are religious or not.

Take Gandhi, for example. He was so captivated with the life and teachings of Jesus that he became one of the greatest followers of Jesus ever. One of the most common descriptions of Gandhi was that he was Christlike. Gandhi discovered that his cultural background as a Hindu was enhanced by Jesus. "I shall say to Hindus," he once said, "that your life will be incomplete unless you reverentially study the teachings of Jesus. . . . Make this world the kingdom of God and his righteousness and everything will be added unto you."[15] Gandhi, whose goal in life was to live the Sermon on the Mount, said, "It was that sermon that has endeared Jesus to me."[16] And, about Jesus' death on the cross, he said, "A man who was completely innocent, offered himself as a sacrifice for the good of others, including his enemies, and became the ransom of the world. It was a perfect act."[17]

And finally the quote that was probably his most famous: "I like your Christ. I do not like your Christians. They are so unlike your Christ."[18]

The current Dalai Lama is another example. He has expressed his love and respect for Jesus in many ways and on many occasions. Many of his teachings reflect those of Jesus. As the example and leader of the Buddhist community, the Dalai Lama is called His Holiness, yet he says he is not worthy to even untie the shoes of Jesus. In an op-ed article he wrote for *The New York Times*, the Dalai Lama said, "In my readings of the New Testament, I find myself inspired by Jesus' acts of compassion. His miracle of the loaves and fishes, his healing and his teaching are all motivated by the desire to relieve suffering."[19]

Both Gandhi and the Dalai Lama revere Jesus as the greatest teacher and example who ever lived. *Son of God or a liar?*

And then there are today's Jews. Some of the most prominent rabbis have come to consider Jesus as possibly the most influential Jew who ever lived. Dr. David Flusser, in his book *The Sage from Galilee*, broke down many barriers that have kept Jews from studying Jesus.[20] Albert Einstein, one of the greatest scientists in the world, said this about Jesus: "As a child, I received instruction both in the Bible and in the Talmud. I am a Jew, but I am enthralled by the luminous figure of the Nazarene. . . . No one can read the Gospels without feeling the actual presence of Jesus. His personality pulsates in every word."[21]

Unfortunately, though, when Jews attempt to study the life and teachings of Jesus, they do so with the weight of history pushing against them. The Jewish people have been so persecuted by people who have called themselves Christians throughout history—from the Crusades to the Holocaust (yes, Hitler was very public about his Christianity)—that it is extremely difficult for them to see Jesus clearly.

Meanwhile, most Christians are unaware that the Muslim holy book, the Qur'an, refers to Jesus more times than it does Muhammad. The prophet Jesus, known as Isa, is held up as the only supernatural prophet. The prophet Jesus is presented as a miracle worker, the "Word of God," the "clear sign of God," born of a virgin, alive today, and coming back to bring peace on earth. Jesus is also identified as the "Ruhallah"—the only one originating from the Spirit of God (Allah). Jesus is viewed as the unique One, who was articulated in the Injil (the Gospels of the Bible).[22]

But when Muslims attempt to study the life and teachings of Jesus, they do so with the weight of history against them too. The ugly history of the Crusades still lingers today. Add to this ugliness the hateful narrative from extremists within the Christian and Muslim communities, and you can see why Jesus' image has become so distorted in many Muslims' eyes.

Agnostics are another group of people who have many in their ranks who follow Jesus. In my experience they are perhaps the most open to Jesus when he is presented without all the religious baggage. Agnostics have a God-shaped vacuum in their hearts. I enjoy conversing with agnostics, once I am able to convince them that I don't want to discuss religion. It seems that this group is better able to view Jesus separated from the religious wrappings. They've already rejected the religious trappings and were left empty. But, when introduced to Jesus without religious baggage, so often they respond by saying, "I can follow *this* Jesus!"

The "self-help movement" is still another group of people who revere Jesus, some going as far as to follow him. Even in our highly educated, secularized society, the principles of Jesus are the basis for most of the self-help and motivational principles. Though they may not use his name, they do use his teaching and his example.

In many ways this is nothing new. Jesus has always worked with people from every culture and found them to be attracted to him. The problem in the first century was the religious jealousy of the gatekeepers of Judaism. When Jesus presented his message of love and compassion to the nonreligious and to all other non-Jewish nations of the world, he was resisted, ridiculed, and ultimately rejected by the Jewish religious leaders of his day.

Why?

Jesus was a threat to their holy huddle.

Sound familiar?

The Most Common Obstacle to Following Jesus

I want to share with you what I believe to be the most common obstacle that discourages people from following Jesus. This obstacle is erected with the use of the popular, almost sacred question "Is Jesus a liar, a lunatic, or Lord?"

He doesn't fit the profile of a liar. He certainly isn't a lunatic. He *must* be Lord.

The logic is irrefutable.

I embraced this logic and taught it for many years to thousands of people. I drew a chart illustrating these three options and said, "Most people avoid these options and think of Jesus as a good teacher or a great example." Then I would move into my most dogmatic voice and say, "He didn't leave that alternative to us! Jesus was either the Lord, a liar, or he was nuts!"

I made fun of anyone who couldn't see this. Then I'd invite people to accept Jesus as the Lord. (I mean, really, who wants to say that Jesus is a liar or a lunatic?) I was really forcing them into this decision by the process of elimination. This happens over and over. People are forced to choose Jesus as Lord! Much like Charlemagne forced the Saxons at the river to choose Jesus as *their* Lord.

Though we don't use lethal force to get a person to make that choice, we often use emotional force or peer pressure. How do we do this? By having people go forward to the altar. By having them pray a prescribed prayer. By encouraging them to stand and say, "I believe!" By suggesting they throw a stick in a campfire. So, by some active response, a person must choose to believe that Jesus is Lord. Whether he knows Jesus or not. Whether he understands what that means or not. I excluded so many who couldn't make the jump over the hurdle to believe Jesus was the Lord.

Most people don't take a running start and leap like a long jumper into accepting Jesus as Lord. Most people can't do that. Most of us come to Jesus in steps. And we follow him in steps too. We all, then, need and deserve to be able to ask questions, to discover, to learn about Jesus at our own pace.

What I should have said to people is what Philip said to Nathanael and what the woman at the well said to the people in her village: "Come and see."[23] *Come and see what?*

Jesus himself never pressured anyone with these tent-revival tactics. He never required anyone to believe he was Lord. He never required anyone to believe he was the Son of God. He never required anyone to believe he was the Messiah.

That just wasn't his approach. *That Jesus in Lord*

His approach was simply to say, "Come."

"Come to me."

"Come and follow."

"Come and rest."

"Come and learn."

So, why do so many of us insist on placing hurdles in the way of people checking Jesus out?

Honoring the Curiosity

Jesus' early followers were curious about Jesus, impressed with his teaching, and drawn to his example. As they followed him, they heard and saw wonderful things, amazing things even. They heard him give the Sermon on the Mount. They saw him change water into wine. They watched as he healed the sick and fed the hungry. They were highly responsive to him at first, but they weren't strong believers at the beginning of the journey. But, step by step, they came closer to him, saw more, heard more. And step by step, they were changing, something was stirring in them. The kindness of God. The Kingdom of God. Such wonderful things, new things, life-giving things.

You see, there are lots of people (maybe you are one of them) who are just where the disciples were in the beginning—curious, fascinated, interested in this Jesus, impressed even.

When I tell an interested agnostic that he is exactly like the early disciples of Jesus, he or she is taken aback. But this is true! They are leaning in to get to know more about Jesus. What happens to this interest if the door is shut in their faces by forcing them to believe certain things without examination?

So, Who Can Follow Jesus?

In a word—anyone!

And *how* can we follow him?

There seem to be three progressive stages of following Jesus.

First, people follow Jesus because he is genuine and winsome. He is the one Person who has truly walked the walk, and walked it perfectly. No one argues with this. There is nothing wrong with this type of following Jesus at all. This is following the pattern of the early disciples or followers.

Second, as people continue to follow this winsome and attractive Jesus, many begin to resonate with his life—the way he talks, the things he says, the way he treats people. They resonate with his love, his compassion, his gentleness, his mercy. Something inside them resounds with the truth of his teachings, the simplicity of his illustrations, and the sincerity of his spirit. They find Jesus not only practical and meaningful to their lives; they find him admirable and exemplary.

Third, as people continue to follow this Jesus and find his teachings meaningful, they may come to the point of realizing he is more than just another human. Many find peace through Jesus—peace within themselves and peace with others. Many find a joy that continues, no matter what's happening around them. Many find Jesus as a reference point, bringing them balance and perspective. Many find a hope in Jesus that gets them through the trials in life. Many find that Jesus satisfies their deepest longings and dreams. Many find Jesus someone they can talk to and get real answers impressed in their hearts. Many see Jesus as a great prophet. Many see Jesus as God with skin on.

The continuum of following Jesus is illustrated best in an encounter

Jesus had with Peter and his early followers in a place called Caesarea Philippi. They had been following this attractive, irresistible, and relevant Jesus for quite some time, and now the question came from Jesus: "Who do you say I am?"[24]

Peter's answer was "You are the Messiah, the Son of the living God."[25] This was the first time any of the disciples had expressed this view with a sense of conviction. The thought had been there, but now Peter seemed to nail it down. And the others seemed to agree. They believed Jesus was God's Messiah, the Son of the living God.

Now note Jesus' reply to Peter's answer. He first said, "Blessed are you, Simon son of Jonah." Jesus stroked Peter for expressing this answer to the question. But before Peter got too puffed up for coming up with this great answer, Jesus quickly said, "This was not revealed to you by flesh and blood."[26]

Do you get that? No human being could have taught this kind of thing to Peter in such a way that it became a part of his deepest convictions. There was no set of doctrines or beliefs that could have brought him to this point. Jesus went on to explain, "but by my Father in heaven." God revealed this to you, Peter.

Why did God reveal this to him?

Because he had been following after this Jesus for years.

To repeat: *anyone, anywhere* can start following after this Jesus.

Can you see that anyone can start following Jesus, no matter what he or she believes, no matter their cultural background, religious background, socioeconomic background, or moral background?

Can you see how Christians, Muslims, Jews, Hindus, Buddhists, Sikhs, agnostics, or people of any other bent may start following Jesus at any point of understanding?

Once an atheist (and a very closed-minded one at that), Oxford professor and critic C. S. Lewis became a follower of Jesus. Reluctantly at first, by his own admission. But he saw enough of this winsome Jesus to take a halting step. One step after the other. Until at last he started thinking differently, living differently, teaching differently, and writing differently. He went from writing essays on literary criticism to writing the *Chronicles of Narnia*. And he remained a follower to the end of his life.

When Lewis was an atheist, Jerry Root reports he made the statement "How absurd that a human could possibly believe that he could have a relationship with the Creator God." He said, "It is as absurd as Hamlet thinking he could have a personal relationship with Shakespeare, his creator."[27]

Later, on further thought, Lewis observed, "Hamlet could have had a personal relationship with Shakespeare, if Shakespeare had written himself, the author/creator, as a character into the play."[28]

This is what I believe God did.

He wrote himself into the play.

The name of the character?

Jesus.

Come and See

Consider this Jesus who is revered as

- the Christ to Christians
- a rabbi to the Jews
- a prophet to the Muslims
- an avatar to the Hindus

• an Enlightened One to Buddhists

• a wise teacher to secularists

• a friend to the broken and disenfranchised.

However they view him, however *you* view him, his name is Jesus. And he is out to deliver the message of good news to all people of all religions, even to those with no religion at all. Here are three of their stories.

A story from a Buddhist: A broken, addicted, and lost Tibetan youth, after studying Jesus three hours a day in a mentoring house, said this: "My life has been changed through getting to know Jesus. I am no longer trapped by my drugs. I have found a family here at the house and am learning to follow Jesus as my Master, even as a Buddhist."

A letter from a Hindu:

Dear Tim,

Your thoughts on Jesus have been thrilling, inspiring and encouraging! It has indeed been a fascinating journey to go through your beautifully crafted articles on Jesus. I think it is mainly because I am a Hindu who follows Jesus wholeheartedly and with joy I accept Him as my redeemer and one and only God! I have always loved Jesus so I got to know about Him some years ago but not the Christianity. I follow His principles and words and try to live accordingly.

I agree with you that one must let his/her family know about Jesus first and then to start one to one with colleagues and gradually to reach everyone with the good news! I have been trying that because I found a great joy in doing so. My wife is still an orthodox Hindu, but she does not have a problem in loving Jesus. I am confident that one day she will have a new life in Jesus. I tell you, like many other Hindus, she does not like Christianity.

Since 1951, right after the "Ranas" downfall in Nepal, Christians started pouring in to Nepal in different names to convert people into another civilization, Christianity. I think that was the serious mistake! It is just an analysis, perhaps I am wrong. Today there are just about a million Christians in Nepal (predominantly a Hindu country) but honestly telling there are very few true followers of Jesus. I wish more were here, telling people that Jesus is not only for Christians, but for all, regardless of their cultural and religious identities.

I believe you are aware that most of the pastors of the Churches in this country are rich and are living a lavish life! People here call them emerging Christian businessmen as they continue to flourish with generous aid from the West. Every year thousands of dollars enters in this country in the name of building churches and serving the poor. We must pray for these brothers and sisters that they come to know Jesus and repent what they have been doing. We also need to pray for them that they begin to follow Jesus!

But, what does it mean to them to follow Jesus?

A story from a Muslim family: My wife, Diana, and I have had the privilege of meeting with Muslim students and other young Muslims over the years. One of our most thrilling experiences occurred when we met with a Muslim family.

The women were all covered. These were serious Muslims. I shared with them that we have been diligently following Jesus and that this journey has led us to find Jesus in their Holy Book, the Qur'an. They knew Jesus was in the Qur'an, and so they were pleased with my words. I shared with them that Jesus is the only supernatural prophet within the Qur'an, the only one who performed miracles. They readily agreed with me as I continued to tell them what we've found about Jesus in the Qur'an.[29]

I continued by sharing with them that Jesus is called the "word of God" several times in the Qur'an. Jesus was identified as the "clear sign" of God, which equates to being the "way to God." Again, they agreed with my analysis about Jesus, though I'm convinced they had never heard such things before. They also had never met anyone who was actually following Jesus as if Jesus were actually alive and real. To them, anyone who claimed to follow Jesus in this way was a Christian who was interested in converting them to Christianity . . . *until* they met us. They loved hearing about this Jesus and are eager to talk more about this Jesus and how to follow him.

My point in sharing these stories with you is to say that people around the world are eager to come and see, not Christianity, not the Church, but *Jesus*. And when you show them *just* Jesus, without all the cultural and ecclesiastical add-ons, they are drawn to him.

I come to you without credentials or qualifications, more like the woman at the well than the leader of the religious council. I come with a simple but sincere plea: Come see. Come see this man who can't be explained, can't be put into a box, can't be categorized, systematized, or Christianized.

It doesn't matter where you are from—America, Asia, Africa. It doesn't matter who you are—male or female, rich or poor, gay or straight.

It doesn't matter what you do—salesperson, agricultural worker, teacher. It doesn't matter if you are a part of the system of Christianity, the system of some other religion, or no religion at all.

"Come," Jesus says. "Come to me. And come as you are."

Does it matter if you are a
Committed unrepentant sinner?
Jesus does not condem
but says - "go and sin
nomore"

CHAPTER 4

Blinders Off

Growing up, I was not only Christian; I was a *Baptist* Christian. And I was not just any kind of Baptist. I was a General Association of Regular Baptists. I attended a Christian liberal arts university. Then I made my way through the labyrinth of a four-year theological seminary. I logged seven years of Greek in order to study the New Testament. I spent three and a half years learning Hebrew in order to study the Old Testament. I learned so much there. In fact, most of what I learned I've never been able to share with anyone, because no one has asked me a question about it. This is why I say I've been educated beyond my intelligence.

Although I discovered that quite a few more than I ever thought are getting into heaven (even Methodists and Catholics!), very little time at seminary was given to either practical ministry training or learning how to think. A few of our teachers had a refreshing way of provoking thought, but that was rare. For the most part we were indoctrinated into a certain ideology—an unswerving theological point of view—without the opportunity to question or disagree. Seminary was more like a vocational training school. Like so much of our educational experience today, the process was to take notes and burp them back up on the bluebook exam. When I was handed my diploma, I also received, unknown to me at the time, a set of Western Christian blinders.

Have you seen racehorses wearing blinders on a racetrack? They serve a purpose—to keep the horses focused. The blinders I had received served to keep me focused too. Focused on what I had been taught, on reading and listening to the fraternity of those who thought as we did, giving me the ability to argue our form of Christianity, convincing me that I had the truth and that truth must be spread.

I learned the art of add-ons. I learned how to substitute Christianity, Church, and charisma for Jesus. I learned how to leave him out of most of my conversations and out of most of my life. My life was filled with Christianity. Studying it. Teaching it. Defending it. Spreading it.

Looking back, I see that my vocational training didn't mentor me in following Jesus.

The goal was to be a good Dallas man who could be counted on to "preach the Word." With a few exceptions along the way, I didn't encounter Jesus. But I did encounter Christianity, at least my theological corner of it.

In college, I had been trained in classical rhetoric; in seminary, I had listened to and been mentored by the best orators there. The more I worked with my audiences, the more I grappled with people's personal problems and relational entanglements. I learned to scratch where people itched, and people itched a lot. The more they itched, the more I scratched. Although the principles I was using were taught by Jesus, I presented them more subtly in the manner of self-help. I had learned to work for Jesus in an advisory capacity, even though there were no openings or positions like that available. Vocationally, I was viewed as a success. Thousands were showing up every weekend. Thousands upon thousands were buying my books. I had as many speaking engagements as I wanted. And a waiting list of people who wanted me to counsel them.

Where I Missed the Point

Fitted with my vocational blinders, and living in the spotlight of my status as a Christian celebrity, I missed the point of Jesus. I couldn't see him. I missed his teachings. I missed the significance of his actions. I missed Jesus, simply Jesus.

My vocational blinders had me highly motivated to prepare a great message for the weekend Church show. After all, if the weekend show (where we spent most of our budget) didn't go well, everything else suffered. Therefore, I did not spend most of my time in preparing my heart or in researching the teachings of Jesus (I thought I already knew about Jesus!). I spent most of my time in packaging the message in such a way as to dazzle the crowd. And it worked!

Most of the time, though, Jesus was left behind.

Our success seduced us. And we missed the revolutionary nature of Jesus, who had no desire to build a holy huddle and keep it together. We came each Sunday to build the huddle—and Jesus came to break it up!

My particular story isn't the point, except as an illustration. The point is that all of us have blinders that keep us from seeing anything more than a sliver of who Jesus is. But over time, with work and determination, we can begin to see Jesus more nearly as he really is. Converting others to our holy huddle is not what really matters. What matters is having a relationship with Jesus.

Jesus' Huddle-Breaking Encounters

When I began to look at Jesus with a new perspective, I discovered that he made a habit of reaching out to people from all kinds of religious and cultural backgrounds. He was inclusive, not exclusive, as is so often taught. My vocational, religious blinders kept me from seeing this all-inclusive Jesus in action.

Let's examine three encounters Jesus had with people from other nations. These are great illustrations of how he was about breaking up holy huddles and reaching out to all cultures.

The woman at the well. One day, on his way from Jerusalem to Galilee, Jesus took a shortcut through Samaria. This was not the usual route Jews would take, because they were locked up in major tension with the Samaritans. The Jews rejected the Samaritans and kept separate from them. The reason? Samaritans were a mixed race and not as pure as the Jews. The animosity between the two was intense. No trust, no association, not even conversation.

While traveling through Samaria, Jesus and his disciples stopped at the well at the town of Sychar. Jesus decided to rest at the well, but his disciples went into town to shop for food. It was noon, the hottest time of the day, and a woman showed up to draw water. Jesus initiated a conversation with her, asking for a drink. She was shocked that he, a Jew, would even speak to her.

In the course of the conversation, he turned her attention to a special kind of water—living water. He explained that living water is different from well water. Sure, well water quenches physical thirst, but living water quenches the thirst of the soul. He told her that this living water is so satisfying that she would never thirst again. In fact, this living water becomes a whole well of water within that springs up to eternal life.

Naturally, she wanted this kind of water. Who wouldn't?

Then Jesus got personal. He told her to go and get her husband.

She said, "I have no husband."

Jesus replies, "You are right. You've had five husbands and are working on the sixth!"[30]

With this incredible insight into her life, the woman believed Jesus must be some kind of prophet. So she turned the discussion toward religion and their differences in worship.

Jesus' response is unique: "Woman, believe me, a time is coming when you will not worship God in your Samaritan way nor in the Jewish way. Soon true worshipers of God will worship in spirit and in truth, not in a certain building or location. God is looking for people to seek him this way, since God is Spirit and Truth."[31]

The woman expressed that she knew God would be sending his Messiah and he would explain all things.

That is when Jesus made a shocking, some would say scandalous declaration: "I am he."[32]

At that moment the disciples showed up to see their Jewish leader alone with a Samaritan woman. She quickly left for town to share about this strange yet wonderful encounter. She told her neighbors, "Come, see a man who told me everything I ever did! Could this be the Messiah?"[33]

The townspeople came to the well to see Jesus for themselves. They urged him to stay with them, and he stayed with them for two days. Many others believed, the text says, based on what he shared with them.[34]

Note what happened here. Jesus shifted the discussion of well water to living water. He was interested in this woman and her life. Jesus already knew her, and he accepted her anyway. That blew her mind! Jesus wanted to show her how to be truly satisfied in a new way. He didn't argue religious or cultural differences. He pointed her to true worship of God in the heart. Jesus didn't make any move to convert her to another religious system. He was offering a personal relationship with God, not an opportunity to change huddles.

The woman from Syrophoenicia. Exhausted by the many arguments he was having with the religious leaders, Jesus left the area for a getaway in the region of Tyre and Sidon, a non-Jewish area. In the home where Jesus was to stay he encountered a non-Jewish woman. Mark calls her Syrophoenician, and Matthew refers to her as Canaanite. Whatever name is used, her people were not friendly to the Jews.

The Syrophoenicians or Canaanites worshiped a variety of nature gods. The chief god, El, was portrayed as a bully, and this image kept people in fear. The woman with this religious background boldly asked Jesus for help. Her daughter was tormented by evil spirits. Since her gods hadn't helped, the mother now turned to Jesus. He initially dismissed her request, but her persistence won out.

Jesus said to her, "You have great faith! Your request is granted."[35] Her daughter was healed that very hour.

Note what happened here. Jesus honored her faith. He didn't pull her into a new religious system, didn't invite her to join a study class, didn't urge her to renounce her cultural upbringing, didn't warn her of the many man-made myths and gods of her religion.

This woman sought and received, and now she had her daughter whole. As a result, she went away with a special relationship with Jesus that she would never forget.

Why didn't Jesus try to convert her to the one true God and pull her away from El or polytheism—the many gods? Why didn't Jesus invite her into the "holy huddle" of Judaism? Didn't he care about keeping the holy huddle holy? Or at least keeping the holy huddle a huddle?

The Roman Centurion

When Jesus had entered Capernaum, a centurion came to him, asking for help. "Lord," he said, "my servant lies at home paralyzed, suffering terribly."

Jesus said to him, "Shall I come and heal him?"

The centurion replied, "Lord, I do not deserve to have you come under my roof. But just say the word, and my servant will be healed. For I myself am a man under authority, with soldiers under me. I tell this one, 'Go,' and he goes; and that one, 'Come,' and he comes. I say to my servant, 'Do this,' and he does it."

When Jesus heard this, he was amazed and said to those following him, "Truly I tell you, I have not found anyone in Israel with such great faith."[36]

Now, wait a minute, Jesus! This non-Jewish, Roman centurion has greater faith than you've seen in Israel? Really? But he has no religious training. How can this be?

Jesus not only pronounced a non-Jew the greatest man of faith he had seen in Israel; he rubbed it in harder. Jesus went on to say, "Many will come from the east and the west, and will take their places at the feast with Abraham, Isaac, and Jacob in the kingdom of heaven. But the subjects of the

Jesus sees our hearts.

kingdom will be thrown outside."[37] Those who you wouldn't think would be in God's Kingdom will be. And those you would think will surely be in the Kingdom will not be.

"Then Jesus said to the centurion, 'Go! Let it be done just as you believed it would.'"[38] And the centurion's servant was healed that very moment.

Again, we need to pay attention and note what happened here—and what didn't. Jesus didn't warn the Roman centurion to avoid the many Roman gods. Jesus' concern was his faith. Jesus didn't urge this man to repent and renounce the Roman deities or his faith would not be effective.

Why was Jesus repeatedly affirming the faith of people from other nations?

Why was Jesus repeatedly exposing the lack of faith of the religious holy huddle?

All three of these encounters with Jesus—and several more like them that I could name—were with people from other nations. They were not within the Jewish holy huddle. In fact, Jesus used each of these to break up the huddle and to blow up the spirit of exclusivity that tends to rise up within such huddle.

A Huddle-Breaker for Me

Several years ago I had the privilege of speaking to an international gathering hosted by the Dalai Lama. Over five hundred clerics—Muslim, Jewish, Hindu, Christian, and Buddhist—were invited by His Holiness to discuss peace and compassion.

The American Buddhist who called to invite me shared with me the purpose of the upcoming gathering: to establish a multireligious body that would work to quell violence and promote harmony among people of different faiths. Then he said, "We want to invite you to speak at this event. We have two Christians who will be representing Christianity, and we feel we need one more."

I said, "I don't have to speak. I would just love to attend this special event. Besides, I am not a good representative of Christianity. I just don't do that very well."

Stunned, my new Buddhist friend asked, "What do you represent?"

"I'm just a stubborn follower of Jesus," I replied. "He is the only one I am comfortable representing."

He sat silently on the phone for several seconds and said, "You know, I think that's better!"

Quickly I said, "I do too!"

With that, I was officially invited to sit on the platform with the Dalai Lama and at some point to speak.

The Gathering of Hearts Illuminating Compassion was held at the Intercontinental Mark Hopkins Hotel in San Francisco. All of the speakers were seated on the platform. I confess my anxiety level was high in anticipation of what I was going to say. The audience also seemed to have some anxiousness. It was in the air.

Then the Dalai Lama entered the room from the back, along with several monks. The monks took seats on the front row, and His Holiness made his way to the platform to sit right in the middle of the speakers. When he sat down, he removed his sandals, crossed his legs, sat back, and giggled as he looked out over the audience. That giggle broke the tension.

The Dalai Lama opened the session with words of gratitude to the representatives of various faiths and cultures gathered together, noting that this conference was only the beginning of many more gatherings "where we may find a gathering of hearts to bring peace to our world."

After his words of greeting, we heard from a variety of speakers (Muslim, Hindu, Jewish, Christian, and Buddhist), beginning with the well-known author of *The World's Religions*, Huston Smith.

So many thoughts raced through my mind about what I should say. What was most striking to me was the absence of the name of Jesus during the three hours of speakers, even from those who were designated to represent Christianity.

After sitting on the edge of my chair through the entire session, I was briefly introduced. I was the last speaker of the day before His Holiness was to close our time together.

I just knew this was the best spot in the program to bring up the only one in history who could provide peace for any who wanted it. So I began with "I bring you greetings in the name of Jesus."

The shock wave we all experienced at the mention of the name of Jesus was one of the most dramatic encounters with Jesus I've ever sensed.

I continued, "Since Jesus is not owned by Christians or Christianity, not bound by any system of dos and don'ts, not exclusive but all-inclusive in his approach to people everywhere (he will work with anyone!), then it is appropriate to bring greetings in his name at this great event. In following Jesus I have come to realize that what the world needs now is not more love."

I paused for a moment so that the audience could digest these words, because most of what had been discussed all afternoon was about the need for love in our world. After a pregnant pause, I continued, "What the world needs now is more lovers—love in action."

It was obvious that the audience was in agreement.

I ended my time with "May Jesus fill your hearts and minds with his peace, his joy, his love, his compassion, and may he bind us together in such a way that we might be contagious in making a difference through him in our world."

The applause was not just polite but enthusiastic and animated.

As soon as the session was dismissed, clerics from all faiths flocked to me. They each expressed their enthusiasm for hearing more about Jesus unchained by Western, cultural Christianity.

One American Buddhist rushed up to me, saying, "You're going to Tibet with me!" In further conversation this same man said, "I've never heard about Jesus separated from Christianity. You know, having heard Jesus in this way, I think I see what you are saying. I would say that Jesus trumps everything!"

On that day those words were imprinted indelibly in my heart. That day the last bit of my vocational blinders fell off.

New Playgrounds

How about you? What are you going to do about your own holy huddle, if you have one?

In the world of "Anonymous" groups, they talk about finding new playgrounds and new playmates. If you have a religion addiction, as I do, maybe that's what you need too.

It seems that there are two kinds of holy huddles.

The first kind of holy huddle is the one that has been developed throughout your years of growing up. When Jesus is brought into that huddle, and your playgrounds and playmates are not receptive to this Jesus kind of thinking and teaching, then you must find a way to break out of those structures that are keeping this revolutionary Jesus out. Don't be too quick to remove yourself from your cultural background and "convert" to another culture. That may not be necessary, and it may not prove to be helpful in learning to follow Jesus. Rather, pray for others who are in your culture who are open to following Jesus and his teachings. All you are looking for is one or two others who are leaning in to follow after this Jesus.

The second kind of holy huddle is the huddle that has been formed after you are converted out of your native cultural background. You feel you have been converted out of darkness into light, so you tend to huddle up with those who think alike. If you have come to know Jesus through whatever experience of conversion you've experienced, this is wonderful! However, don't feel as if you are trapped in this new huddle, especially if this particular huddle is becoming more and more exclusive, believing itself to be the only right spiritual huddle around. You might consider returning to your original culture and looking for people there who have found Jesus. (Or more properly, whom Jesus has found.)

Whatever you do, don't allow yourself to be influenced more by your huddle members than by Jesus himself. If Jesus says one thing and your huddle members seem to be saying something different, stick with Jesus!

Jesus is the point. Simply Jesus.

And he trumps everything!

CHAPTER 5

Blessed to Be a Blessing

Two questions are left over from what we've already learned. Two very important questions, the answers to which will change everything.

1. Why was Jesus so intent on breaking up the holy huddles wherever he went?

2. Why did he repeatedly invite those from other nations to himself?

There is a primary reason why Jesus took on the responsibility of breaking up the holy huddle of the Jews. It all goes back to Abraham, the father of monotheism. He was known as the friend of God and was one of the most prominent characters from the beginnings of Judaism, Christianity, and Islam. Abraham's unshakable faith and submission to the one God has served as a major inspiration and example to all three religions.

Even today, many Christians believe they own Jesus in the same way that the Jews believed they owned God and his truth, even his Messiah. The solution for this mistaken attitude, if you or I have it, is to put on our dance shoes.

The Abrahamic Two-Step

According to the Scriptures, God made a covenant with Abram, and there were two parts to it. Here is the way the passage reads in *The Message:*

> I'll make you a great nation
> > and bless you.
> I'll make you famous;
> > you'll be a blessing.
> I'll bless those who bless you;
> > those who curse you I'll curse.
> All the families of the Earth
> > will be blessed through you.[39]

I call this the "Abrahamic two-step."

Step 1: God will bless the people who are faithful to Him.

Step 2: God will be a blessing to all nations of the world through His people.

In the case of the Jewish people, God was going to bless Israel as a nation as long as they were faithful to Him, specifically faithful in being a blessing to the nations of the world!

God even changed Abram, meaning "noble father," to Abraham, which means "the father of many nations." God wanted to bless the whole world through Abraham. God had a bigger vision for Abraham. God was looking for the salvation of the whole world through Abraham. Abraham was to be not only the physical father but also the spiritual father of many nations, aka Gentiles.[40]

Jesus' mission was to break up the Jewish holy huddle that was stuck

God blesses those who are faithful to Him.

in Step 1. So Jesus' encounters with people from the nations of the world were examples of how Step 2 was to be carried out—to be a blessing to the world!

The Jewish holy huddle that Jesus found when he came was in a narrow-minded, rigid, inflexible, dogmatic state of mind. With their blinders on, they were unable to see the big picture of what God was up to. They had ears to hear but couldn't hear. They had eyes to see but couldn't see. And Jesus' early followers had a difficult time opening their eyes and ears!

Jesus Lived Out Abraham's Two-Step

In the last chapter we examined how Jesus fulfilled Step 2 of the Abrahamic two-step as he related to people from the nations of the world. Another powerful example is the time when Jesus became angry with businessmen and threw them out of the Temple.

I've always believed Jesus was upset over the business done in the Temple. And he was. Not just doing business there, but cheating people in the changing of money, in the selling of "more acceptable" animals for sacrifice, in selling all of the religious knickknacks available at the time. But there was more going on.

Through the prophet Isaiah, God directed that the Temple was to be a "house of prayer *for all nations.*"[41] The Temple represented the very presence of God dwelling with his people. Therefore, all people from every nation were to have access to him there. This is why the Jews were directed to have a special place for non-Jews to come to the Temple to worship.

It seems Step 2 of the Abrahamic two-step was a priority neither to the Temple authorities in the first century nor to the Jewish people in general. The holy huddle desired to be kept pure from any contamination. Consequently, they cleared out the Court of the Nations—the place set aside for the non-Jews to worship—and allowed the money changers and vendors to use this "unused" space for business.

Why not? Being a blessing to the nations of the world was not a priority of the huddle!

I think this is the real reason for Jesus' anger. What's interesting is that we've rarely been taught this reason, because being a blessing to the nations of the world is only important if conversion to Christianity is the end game. We tend to keep Jesus exclusively for ourselves and shut out the nations of the world. We'll share Jesus with the nations of the world as the Christian door to God, and we believe Christianity is the way to God.

 Christianity is not the way.

Jesus is!

When you come to the understanding that God is calling people to himself from all of the nations of the earth, you begin to realize he is uniquely already inside their culture, doing his work. We must point out to people in these other cultures of the world what God is doing and how he is working. We must pray for leaders within that culture to have ears to hear and eyes to see.

This kind of global movement is happening today. It's what I call the *Jesus movement*. People from every nation are hearing God's call on their lives and are responding by studying and worshiping Jesus in homes, mosques, temples, and government quarters. Dramatic changes are occurring in the individuals caught up in this movement. They love Jesus and diligently follow his teachings. They don't call themselves Christians and they don't call their gatherings "Churches."

This movement is emerging not from any one religious sect or system. It is a movement of God—and it cannot be stopped! This is what was always intended.

Even the Temple priest who first held Jesus in his arms as a baby knew clearly why Jesus came:

> My eyes have seen your salvation,
>> which you have prepared in the sight of *all nations:*
> a light for revelation to *the Gentiles,*
>> and the glory of your people Israel.[42]

Note the coming of the Messiah was to be a global event, not for one nation but for all nations. The one was a means to the other. A light was given to Israel, and it was to be a city set on a hill, so to speak, shining as a beacon of light to all the nations. Tragically, though, they hid that light by huddling around it themselves and consequently lost sight of their global mission.

Jesus Taught Abraham's Two-Step

Jesus not only acted out Abraham's two-step; he taught Step 2 repeatedly. Jesus was clearly into opening the blindered minds of those who would listen—those who might have ears to truly hear and eyes to truly see. I could cite several stories from the life of Jesus, but let me focus on just a couple.

After Jesus healed a man with a withered hand on the Sabbath, the religious leaders plotted how they might kill him. Aware of this, Jesus withdrew from that place. A large crowd followed him, and he healed all who were ill. Jesus warned them not to tell others about him. Matthew says,

> This was to fulfill what was spoken through the prophet Isaiah:
> "Here is my servant whom I have chosen,
>> the one I love, in whom I delight;
> I will put my Spirit on him,
>> and he will proclaim justice to the *nations*. . . .
>> In his name the *nations* will put their hope."[43]

Another time Jesus taught this concept was in his hometown of Nazareth. This was one of the most anticipated opportunities for Jesus. News of his speaking engagement rapidly spread, and all came to hear him at their local synagogue.

When Jesus showed up on the Sabbath in the synagogue, as a guest rabbi he was asked to recite the reading of the day.

> He stood up to read, and the scroll of the prophet Isaiah was handed to him. Unrolling it, he found the place where it is written:
> "The Spirit of the Lord is on me,
>> because he has anointed me
>> to proclaim good news to the poor.
> He has sent me to proclaim freedom for the prisoners
>> and recovery of sight for the blind,
>> to set the oppressed free,
> to proclaim the year of the Lord's favor."[44]

The home crowd loved it. Little Jesus had made them proud. How amazing it was!

"He rolled up the scroll, gave it back to the attendant, and sat down. The eyes of everyone in the synagogue were fastened on him. . . . [Jesus said,] 'Today this scripture is fulfilled in your hearing.'"[45]

"All spoke well of him," the text says, "and were amazed at the gracious words that came from his lips."[46]

Then the bombshell.

Jesus said, "Truly I tell you, no prophet is accepted in his hometown."[47] He then offered two illustrations of prophets who were not welcomed and how those of other nations were blessed by their famous prophets.

First prophet: Elijah. Jesus said, "I assure you that there were many widows in Israel in Elijah's time, when the sky was shut for three and a half years and there was a severe famine throughout the land. Yet Elijah was not sent to any of them, but to a widow in Zarephath in the region of Sidon."[48] In other words, God sent one of his prophets to a non-Jewish widow who fed and housed him.

Second prophet: Elisha. Jesus went on to say, "And there were many in Israel with leprosy in the time of Elisha the prophet, yet not one of them was cleansed—only Naaman the Syrian."[49] God didn't bless any Jewish lepers with healing, but he did heal a non-Jew.

The people were livid. They rose up, drove Jesus out of town, and took him to the brow of a hill to throw him off the cliff. But, perhaps miraculously, he slipped through the crowd and went on his way.

Just point out God's blessing on non-Jewish nations and watch the holy huddle squirm! I'll never forget when I introduced our Muslim friend as a follower of Jesus to a group of Palestinian Christian youths in

Bethlehem. The shock and gasps around the room were amazing! Talk about squirming! But as we processed this together, they came to understand for the first time ever that Jesus is not a Christian, nor is he owned by Christians. He is the light *of the world*. Not the Western world. The *whole* world. Not the Christian world. The *whole* world.

Can't be more inclusive than that!

How did we miss the point?

Jesus Commanded Abraham's Two-Step

After showing how to live out the second step of Abraham's covenant with God to be a blessing to the nations of the world, and repeatedly teaching it everywhere he went, Jesus made it the primary mission for his early followers. He clearly directed them to follow through on this mission after his death. For years it's been referred to as the Great Commission.

First of all, the term "Great Commission" isn't even in the Bible! This title evolved to fire up the religious world to be givers and goers in order to convert the world to Christianity. So, going, baptizing, and converting the world became the mission of the "Great Commission," even though Jesus' command is simpler and clearer than that—*to make followers of Jesus in all the nations of the world!*

Note Jesus' words: "All authority in heaven and on earth has been given to me. Therefore *go and make disciples of all nations*."[50]

The late Dr. Ralph Winter, a world-famous expert in Christian missions around the world, said, "Jesus didn't come to give the Great Commission; He came to take it back from the Jews who had it for 2000 years and had done nothing with it."[51] Why? Because they continually missed the point! Dr. Winter understood the "Great Commission" as introducing Jesus into the cultures of the world, not converting people out of those cultures into Western Christianity.

Then, after the resurrection and just before Jesus left, he directed his followers to wait in Jerusalem for the Spirit to come upon them: "You will receive power when the Holy Spirit comes on you; and you will be my witnesses in Jerusalem, and in all Judea and Samaria, and *to the ends of the earth.*"[52]

Jesus made it clear what he wanted his followers to do. They were to take the message of Jesus to the nations of the world. So, where is the narrow-minded, exclusive Jesus in this?

When Jesus' Followers Missed the Point—Big Time!

Missing the point and purpose of Jesus did not begin in the organized religious institution as I have always thought. It began with the earliest followers of Jesus, even before the Jesus movement was officially launched! They missed it within a period of a few days in which they experienced the most miraculous adventure anyone could have ever imagined. There seems to be a natural tendency, no matter how much we have seen and heard, to become distracted from the simplicity of Jesus.

Check out these three scenes following one right after the other in Luke 9.

Scene 1. An argument breaks out among the disciples. What is the argument about? Which of them will be viewed as the greatest.

Here's what Luke records: "Jesus, knowing their thoughts, took a little child and had him stand beside him. Then he said to them, 'Whoever welcomes this little child in my name welcomes me; and whoever welcomes me welcomes the one who sent me. For whoever is least among you all is the greatest.'"[53]

What's this all about? After all of the demonstration they had received that Jesus was the preeminent one, they had already missed the point. Jesus was the point, not them or their comparative greatness!

Scene 2. Then the disciples became jealous over seeing another person doing things in the name of Jesus. John said, "Master, we saw someone driving out demons in your name and we tried to stop him, because he is not one of us."[54]

"Do not stop him," Jesus said, "for whoever is not against you is for you."[55]

Here we go again! These early followers of Jesus were caught up in setting up their own holy huddle. The problem was that there was a person doing things in the name of Jesus. Now note this. John said the problem with this person was that he was "not one of us." Do you get it? This guy who was doing terrific things in the name of Jesus just didn't match up, because he was not a member of their little group. Ever heard or seen that attitude? Again, they were missing the point of Jesus. Their little group had become more important to them than Jesus himself!

Scene 3. In another instance Jesus sent out a few of his followers to get things ready in Samaria. Jesus was planning to go through Samaria to teach and heal there. The Samaritans didn't welcome the preparation for Jesus, so James and John asked Jesus, "Lord, do you want us to call fire down from heaven to destroy them?"[56] But Jesus turned and rebuked them.

See how it was getting worse? The disciples were now so miffed at the Samaritans' response that they were actually suggesting they be destroyed. Actually, it's more serious than that. They weren't asking Jesus to call down fire from heaven; they were thinking *they* might call the fire down to destroy the Samaritans! Are you kidding me? These guys had not only missed the point and purpose of Jesus; they were taking on a little personal prominence for themselves.

So there were three separate clashes over secondary matters: first, a clash among the disciples (*Who's the greatest?*); second, a clash between the disciples and other followers of Jesus (*This guy is not one of us!*); and third, a clash between the disciples of Jesus and a group of people from another religious system (*Let's destroy these Samaritans who aren't receptive to our message!*).

All three clashes shared three common characteristics:

Each clash was motivated by the pride of being more "right" than another—all too common among those who claim to be followers of Jesus today.

Each clash was divisive. If you leave Jesus out of the equation of relationships within the Kingdom, you will inevitably experience divisiveness.

Each clash was missing Jesus as the point of it all.

None of these responses was on-message with what these early followers had experienced in their walk with Jesus. They completely missed the point.

Disciples Learning the Two-Step

All too rarely have Jesus' followers implemented Abraham's two-step as Jesus taught and commanded. But in the New Testament there are several examples of when it *did* happen. In fact, the rapid spread of Jesus' fame in those early decades could not have happened otherwise. Let's look at two instances.

Peter at Caesarea. Peter was visiting a friend in the city of Joppa when he had a vision.

> Peter went up on the roof to pray. He became hungry and wanted something to eat, and while the meal was being prepared, he fell into a trance. He saw heaven opened and something like a large sheet being let down to earth by its four corners. It contained all kinds of four-footed animals, as well as reptiles and birds. Then a voice told him, "Get up, Peter. Kill and eat."
>
> "Surely not, Lord!" Peter replied. "I have never eaten anything impure or unclean."
>
> The voice spoke to him a second time, "Do not call anything impure that God has made clean."
>
> This happened three times, and immediately the sheet was taken back to heaven. [57]

While Peter was wondering about the meaning of the vision, some men sent by a God-fearing Roman centurion named Cornelius (who had already received an angelic vision instructing him to seek out Peter) stopped at the gate.

> They called out, asking if Simon who was known as Peter was staying there.
>
> While Peter was still thinking about the vision, the Spirit said to him, "Simon, three men are looking for you. So get up

and go downstairs. Do not hesitate to go with them, for I have sent them."

Peter invited the men into the house to be his guests. The next day Peter started out with them, and some of the believers from Joppa went along. The following day he arrived in Caesarea. Cornelius was expecting them and had called together his relatives and close friends. As Peter entered the house, Cornelius met him and fell at his feet in reverence. But Peter made him get up. "Stand up," he said, "I am only a man myself."

. . . Peter went inside and found a large gathering of people. He said to them, "You are well aware that it is against our law for a Jew to associate with or visit a Gentile [person from another nation]. But God has shown me that I should not call anyone impure or unclean. So when I was sent for, I came without raising any objection. May I ask why you sent for me?"[58]

Cornelius described the message he had received from the angel. Then Peter began to speak: "I now realize how true it is that God does not show favoritism, but accepts *from every nation* the one who fears him and does what is right."[59]

Did you get that? God welcomes all who come, revering him and doing what is right!

Really—*all?*

Really.

Paul in Pisidian Antioch. Paul and his traveling partner Barnabas spoke in the synagogue in a place called Pisidian Antioch, a non-Jewish area in what is now Turkey. The response was so great that they were asked to return the next week. Nearly the whole city showed up to hear their words about Jesus. When the Jewish holy huddle saw the crowds, they were jealous.

> They began to contradict what Paul was saying and heaped abuse on him.
>
> Then Paul and Barnabas answered them boldly: "We had to speak the word of God to you first. Since you reject it and do not consider yourselves worthy of eternal life, we now turn to the Gentiles [people of other nations]. For this is what the Lord has commanded us:
>
> > 'I have made you a light for the Gentiles,
> >
> > > that you may bring salvation to the ends of the earth.'"[60]

In these last lines, they were quoting the prophet Isaiah. Here is a longer version of the passage in the book of Isaiah that they were quoting:

> It is too small a thing for you to be my servant
>
> > to restore the tribes of Jacob
> >
> > and bring back those of Israel I have kept.
>
> I will also make you a light for the Gentiles,
>
> > that my salvation may reach to the ends of the earth.[61]

When the non-Jews in the crowd heard what Paul and Barnabas had to say, they were glad. "The word of the Lord spread through the whole region. But the Jewish leaders incited the God-fearing women of high standing and the leading men of the city [so much that they] stirred up persecution against Paul and Barnabas and expelled them from their region."[62] All was very positive, until the Jews became jealous of God's inclusiveness.

Abraham's two-step is a dance we all should learn. We all should be learning to share Jesus with people from all places and backgrounds without trying to convert them to our own religious persuasion. That path only leads to conflict.

Here's the principle to keep in mind: *Jesus unites. Everything else divides.*

He is the point. And he *alone.*

Self-Examination

Can I get personal for a moment?

Do *you* see Jesus alone as being the point? Or are you missing the point too, like so many people in the days of Jesus and the apostles?

To figure it out, ask yourself this: *Do I feel the need to add something else to Jesus in order to feel good enough about my life and relationship with God?* What to add or not to add ?

Take a moment and take stock.

I think that, if you are honest, you will have to admit there are some, if not many things that you feel more comfortable having along with you when it comes to following Jesus. Identify those things and hold them up to Jesus, so that he may enlighten you and purify you.

As you meditate on the contrast between Jesus plus additives and Jesus alone, ask him to show you how adequate he can be for you.

CHAPTER 6

Add-ons That Subtract

How did Jesus plus nothing become everything *but* Jesus?

And how does it keep happening today?

Jesus identified a primary flaw in the religious system as it was practiced in his place and time. As he saw it, the flaw didn't reside within the people but within the professionals. Jesus strongly criticized the religious leaders for their made-up commandments, meticulous rules, sacred traditions, and man-made teachings that caused them to set aside the commands of God.[63]

Jesus seems to have kept three tensions at the forefront for those who wanted to follow him. These tensions were present in the first century; they are present in Western culture today; and they are present in a variety of ways throughout the cultures of the world.

To get a clearer picture of what was at the core of Jesus' teachings, let's unpack the three primary tensions to which Jesus referred.

Tension 1: Person vs. Program

This tension gets to the heart of living out a lifestyle of Jesus as simply enough. It's the beginning of the process of missing the point of Jesus. It's the source of it all.

"Person vs. program" could perhaps be more accurately described as "inner vs. outer." Jesus went to the heart of the matter in his first seminar—the Sermon on the Mount. The question in the air was "Jesus, how does your teaching differ from what we've been taught?"

Addressing the importance of the Law, right up front Jesus said, "Anyone who sets aside one of the least of these commands and teaches others accordingly will be called least in the kingdom of heaven, but whoever practices and teaches these commands will be called great in the kingdom of heaven. For I tell you that unless your righteousness surpasses that of the Pharisees and the teachers of the law, you will certainly not enter the kingdom of heaven."[64]

The Pharisees and the teachers of the law were extremely religious people, and they showed off that religiosity to all who might see. Was Jesus suggesting that their righteous way of living was not enough?

Yes!

Jesus wasn't pushing for people to put on more religious and super-spiritual shows in order to enter the Kingdom of heaven. Jesus was pushing for his followers to surpass the righteousness of the Pharisees by going internal.

Instead of making your righteousness an external show, make it a matter of the heart!

To surpass the righteousness of the leaders of the day was to focus on the inner life (the internals) rather than the outer life (the externals).

Note Jesus' emphasis when the externalized Pharisees criticized him and his disciples for not washing their hands properly:

> "Are you still so dull?" Jesus asked them. "Don't you see that whatever enters the mouth goes into the stomach and then out of the body? But the things that come out of a person's mouth come from the heart, and these defile them. For out of the heart come evil thoughts—murder, adultery, sexual immorality, theft, false testimony, slander. These are what defile a person; but eating with unwashed hands does not defile them."[65]

And later Jesus said, "Woe to you, teachers of the law and Pharisees, you hypocrites! You are like whitewashed tombs, which look beautiful on the outside but on the inside are full of the bones of the dead and everything unclean. In the same way, on the outside you appear to people as righteous but on the inside you are full of hypocrisy and wickedness."[66]

The program of the religious leaders of Jesus' day had a complicated, hierarchical system to it, just as our religious programs often do today. When Jesus spoke of this, he said,

> Everything they do is done for people to see: They make their phylacteries wide and the tassels on their garments long; they love the place of honor at banquets and the most important seats in the synagogues; they love to be greeted with respect in the marketplaces and to have people call them "Rabbi."
>
> But you are not to be called "Rabbi," for you have only

one Master and you are all brothers. And do not call anyone
on earth "father," for you have one Father, and he is in heaven.
Nor are you to be called "teacher," for you have one Teacher,
the Messiah. The greatest among you will be your servant. For
those who exalt themselves will be humbled, and those who
humble themselves will be exalted.[67]

Person is about the internal over the external.

Program brings with it a system of externals in order to be seen "right."
Which is easier to follow?

It's much easier to follow a program with its lists of dos and don'ts.
Just check it off the list, and before you know it, you're feeling pretty
good about yourself. Maybe a little too good. This is not only deceptive to
those looking on; you deceive yourself if you think you are a little more
"right" than others for following the program.

Maybe one of the most surprising and difficult areas to resolve in
this tension between *Person* and *program* is found in Jesus' words about
the Scriptures. There is no doubt in my mind that the biblical Scriptures teach Jesus throughout. When Jesus joined the two on their way to
Emmaus, "beginning with Moses and all the Prophets, he explained to
them what was said in all the Scriptures concerning himself."[68]

These religious leaders were diligent in following their program of
study, and yet they missed the point of studying the Scriptures; they held
up the Scriptures as the highest authority of all, even higher than Jesus.
Please don't misunderstand. I believe in the authority of the Scriptures.
However, I hold Jesus up as the highest authority of all—the name above
all names.

Let me illustrate it this way.

If your spiritual leader says one thing and Jesus says something different, who are you going to go with? Jesus!

If you believe something strongly and then find that Jesus doesn't teach it or teaches it differently, who are you going to go with? I'd suggest Jesus.

If your religious system practices one thing and Jesus teaches it differently, who are you going to go with? Of course, Jesus!

If your religious teachings and traditions teach one thing and Jesus teaches it differently, who are going to go with? This may be much tougher, but following Jesus' teaching is the way to go.

Now, if Paul says or emphasizes one thing and Jesus seems to say or emphasize something different, who are you going to go with? This may be one of the toughest choices of all. We have placed such great emphasis on Paul's theological systems that have primarily fashioned the religious system of Christianity—and the core teachings of Jesus have become buried under all of the theology. I'd still strongly encourage you to go with Jesus! *Paul vs. Jesus ?*

At best, this first tension leaves Jesus on the sidelines; at worst, it leaves him behind. *Where & What ?*

The Program Problem Today

The same tension between program and Person exists in our day. People love to be seen as being spiritual by virtue of actions they've been taught in their culture, religious upbringing, or associations. To be seen going to Church, to be identified as a member of a certain Church, to be perceived as one who is really caught up in his worship, to impress others with holier-sounding prayers, to seek recognition for giving generously to the Church, to be known by the leadership of the Church, to sit in the more prominent seats at the gathering—all these and more are things that pull us away from focusing on the Person of Jesus.

Jesus never urged anyone to go to Church or be a member of a Church. Jesus warned against showing off in front of others to be noticed by them as a more spiritual person, especially when it comes to praying, giving, or sitting in the best seats.

Personally, I am distracted away from a Jesus focus when the worship leader, a member of the worship team, or a choir member is dramatically acting out his or her emotions. I love to worship in a gathering with great, meaningful music. I am not drawn to worship God when I am distracted by someone up front putting on a show. Much of this acting out is a learned leadership pose, and those who do it may not realize that this style of leading worship can distract from the real purpose of worship. My son, Tim Timmons Jr., a musician and worship leader, has taught me so much about genuine, heartfelt worship as he leads the gathering into that focus.

Furthermore, when program wins out over Person, you will notice it within the organizational structures. Certain positions are perceived to be more sacred—more holy—than others. For instance, sometimes the leader up front at a gathering—the pastor, the priest, the rabbi, the imam, the teacher—is viewed as being more spiritual than the other worshipers and even having greater access to God. The model of Jesus is that each follower has the same resources and power as the others. The giftedness varies—you certainly don't want a person in the position of teaching who does not know what he or she is talking about—but the spiritual status or access is all the same.

Maybe the up-front positioning of spiritual leaders is wrong thinking and causes everyone else in the group to become spectators and not participators. If the spiritual leader were perceived as a follower of Jesus among other followers of Jesus, rather than having the august position of being the leader who knows all, then maybe the group would become more empowered to actually practice the teachings and principles of Jesus within the context of the community of other followers. I am learning that as I get out of the way instead of doing all of the talking, all of the teaching, and all of the leading, others within the group step up and experience teaching and leading themselves. What a thrill to see this happen!

When I was the pastor, the thinking was that I was the one who should be counseling, encouraging, and praying for the hurting people. It's the pastor's job! It occurred to me one day that anyone who cares can show up at the hospital, place their hands on the sick person's head with the same power of Jesus that I know. The power is not in the program that promotes the position of pastor but in the Person of Jesus.

Tension 2: Relationship vs. Religion

This tension picks up where Tension 1 left off. In Person versus program, the issue is who you are to follow and obey. Tension 2 has more to do with the *how* of authentically following Jesus of Nazareth. It's clear to me that it is impossible to follow God. This is why Jesus, the man, was sent to flesh God out for us to follow. It is a relational lifestyle, not a religious one.

Nothing better illustrates this core relational dynamic than what Jesus teaches as the greatest commandment. The greatest commandment is to love God or relate to God with all your heart, mind, and strength and to love your neighbor as yourself. Jesus didn't even boil it down to one commandment, but taught the greatest commandment as a dynamic relational couplet. According to Jesus, the greatest commandment is the relational foundation for the Law and the Prophets, the power to really live and to find yourself operating as close to the Kingdom as you can.[69]

Jesus' revolutionary call, "Follow me," is always within the context of a relationship. The real tension occurs when a person is invited into a relationship with Jesus and then is taught how to follow a religious system of dos and don'ts. Authentic and meaningful life will never come through a religious system but only within a life-sustaining relationship with Jesus.

Don't miss this: the only way Jesus reveals himself, or works with us, is personally! Never impersonally as a force or energy, as an idea or cause, as a fix or a cure. This relational context with the Person of Jesus is revolutionary! Even for Christians!

A good example is when Jesus extended his call to Matthew: "As Jesus went on from there, he saw a man named Matthew sitting at the tax collector's booth. 'Follow me,' he told him, and Matthew got up and followed him."[70]

The call "Follow me" is all about relationship, not religion. Jesus never says, "Follow a set of rules." It's "Follow me!" It's not, "Get your act together and follow me!" It's not, "Become religious and follow me!" It's not, "Do something to earn God's acceptance and follow me!'

Consider Matthew: a despised tax collector, a traitor to his people because of working for the Romans, a nonreligious loser who never made the grade to follow a rabbi as a kid—now Jesus, the most popular new rabbi on the scene, approaches Matthew with an air of "I accept you as you are. Now follow me!"

No doubt Matthew had been exposed to Jesus' teachings along the seashore and was attracted to him as so many were. Now, to be personally approached by Jesus was mind-boggling to him. He must have felt the love and acceptance, because he quickly responded. He probably called his family and friends right away and invited them all to his house to celebrate.

"While Jesus was having dinner at Matthew's house, many tax collectors and sinners came and ate with him and his disciples. When the Pharisees saw this, they asked his disciples, 'Why does your teacher eat with tax collectors and sinners?'"[71] This is the best thing about tabletop fellowship in a private home. You get to meet many of the family and friends in the process. Matthew's friends were other tax collectors and sinners (the nonreligious). When the religious saw this, they began to grumble. *Get out of the church*

This sets up two of the most amazing teachings of Jesus. Hearing their grumbling, he said, "It is not the healthy who need a doctor, but the sick."[72] He first made it clear that he came to call the sinners, the nonreligious, the spiritually disenfranchised—and not the righteous—into relationship with him. *Witness to sinners*

Jesus went on to clarify this with a fascinating statement: "But go and learn what this means: 'I desire mercy, not sacrifice.' For I have not come to call the righteous, but sinners."[73] *Fellowship with pagans*

Wasn't it God who set up the elaborate sacrificial system for the Jews to follow? Yet it was God who first said this through the ancient prophet, Hosea:

> I desire mercy [a heart of compassion], not sacrifice,
> and acknowledgement of God rather than burnt offerings.[74]

Jesus quoted these words from Hosea and resolved the tension between relationship and religion. Relationship gets God's vote every time! In his eyes, mercy is better than sacrifice, and knowledge of him is better than burnt offerings.

This is good news to those who are religiously out of it, under the guilt pile, or behind in their religious duties, and it's annoying news to those who have performed the sacrificial system flawlessly.

The Religion Problem Today

It would be great if the problem of following religion instead of following Jesus were buried back in the first century. But sadly, it is alive and well today. Of all the true examples I could give to illustrate the way that religious, man-made structures get in the way of a person simply following after Jesus, let me mention just two.

The "wrong" Bible. A young woman who grew up Buddhist expressed an interest in attending a Bible study in her neighborhood. She shared this interest with her employer. He suggested that she go to a bookstore and purchase a Bible, begin reading the five Gospels (Matthew, Mark, Luke, John, and Acts), then begin attending this study she had been invited to join.

At the bookstore she bought a paraphrased version of the Bible, *The Message.* She enthusiastically showed up at the study. It wasn't long though, before the leader of the group—in front of the entire group—gave her to understand that she had not purchased a real Bible and that this version was not acceptable in the group.

You know the end of the story. She was so embarrassed and discouraged that she never went back and has given up the idea of attending such a study altogether for now.

The ugly face of religiosity pushes people away from a personal relationship with Jesus.

The "wrong" path to marriage. The second illustration may be uglier still. A young couple who were living together without marriage had a baby. This new little one motivated them to get back to a spiritual base they had left, and they started attending a local megachurch near where they live.

Their hearts were stirred toward spiritual growth. They went through membership class, were baptized, and joined a small group.

But that's not all. They were on fire spiritually and felt they needed to get married, so they went to the pastor who had baptized them (without knowing they were unmarried) and made their request.

His response was severe. He said that in order for them to keep their Church membership, they must separate for six months, step out of the small group, and get some counseling for their new marriage. They were bruised and broken by this ugly religious rejection.

When we heard of this, we sent to them a person who could love them and bring them along in their spiritual journey. This couple and their entire family experienced the loving and healing touch of Jesus through this move of acceptance. They were married, relocated into a Church where a loving community is valued, and are enjoying their spiritual walk with Jesus and his followers.

Tension 3: Majors vs. Minors

This tension is concerned with the emphasis we place on what's important. For those who follow after *program* rather than the *Person*, for those who follow after *religion* rather than *relationship*, there is a tendency to struggle with what's most important. It's a tendency to major in the minors and minor in the majors.

The religious leaders in the first century were some of the most religious people ever. Their religiosity was all about external matters—separation from sin and sinners and cleansing oneself. They were known for professing righteousness without possessing it, for being hypercritical hairsplitters and theological nitpickers, and for emphasizing the letter of the Law over the spirit of the Law. All truth and little grace. Making absolutes out of the limited. Lists and lists of rules and regulations!

These hypercritical, super-spiritual people are still around today. In fact, I saw one with a bullhorn outside a Dalai Lama gathering, condemning all who were attending, informing us that we were all going to hell!

Because of their diligence in majoring in the minors and minoring in the majors, the Pharisees delighted in pointing out where Jesus' followers kept coming up short. For example, one time they criticized his disciples for not following the detailed washing rituals that the religious leaders required.

Jesus replied like this:

Isaiah was right when he prophesied about you hypocrites; as it is written:

"These people honor me with their lips,
but their hearts are far from me.

They worship me in vain;

their teachings are merely human rules."

You have let go of the commands of God and are hold-ing on to human traditions.[75]

But Jesus wasn't done yet.

He continued: "You have a fine way of setting aside the commands of God in order to observe your own traditions! . . . Thus you nullify the word of God by your tradition that you have handed down. And you do many things like that."[76]

Later, Jesus railed against these religious hypocrites when he said, "Woe to you, teachers of the law and Pharisees, you hypocrites! You give a tenth of your spices—mint, dill and cumin. But you have neglected the more important matters of the law—justice, mercy and faithfulness. You should have practiced the latter, without neglecting the former. You blind guides! You strain out a gnat but swallow a camel."[77]

The Culting Process

Program versus Person. Religion versus relationship. Minors versus majors. Jesus was most concerned with these tensions in the first century. These were serious problems then and they are now! These tensions are at the core of what gets in the way of following Jesus as simply enough.

These tensions end up creating list after list of add-ons. I think it begins with the religious professionals. Over the years they have wanted to show how much more knowledgeable they are by inventing more and more ideas, concepts, rules, and sacraments that they claim to be at the core of the religious system. It's what scientists and educators do to prove their credentials. They are driven to complicate things rather than to simplify them. They earn their credentials by being the ones who claim to understand all of the complexities—things we mere mortals could never really grasp on our own.

When I first seriously studied Jesus' words, I began to see how my religious expression of Christianity had been buried in a myriad of layers that produced a man-made effect.

For instance, as I've said, I grew up as a Baptist. All of our particular brand of Baptist believed and practiced the same things. No dancing! No movies! No drinking! No smoking! Jesus was quite incidental to the lifestyle we were taught to live.

We were all afraid. Afraid of the possibility of going to hell. Afraid of God's judgment on our lives. Afraid of anyone knowing our broken-ness—*truly* knowing us. Afraid of being caught sinning. Afraid of Jesus returning. Afraid of being left behind when he did return.

We weren't a cult, but we were caught up in what I call the "culting" process. We were buried under the many layers of cultural traditions, man-made commandments, social causes, and concerns. The culting process is based upon the desire to be "right," at least more right than others around us. These layers of add-ons succeeded in producing a counterfeit of the real thing.

We had a "Church Covenant" on the right wall of the Church. As a kid, I stared at it often. There were ten things on the list that we couldn't do if we wanted to go to heaven—no dancing, no movies, no alcohol, no sex outside marriage, just to name a few. I found this list to be depress-ing, because as I contemplated them, I realized seven of the ten were my goals in life!

How the Culting Process Works

The culting process is all about *control*, *shortcuts*, and *reformation*.

Control is a common problem among humans. Most cultures of the world have a "garden" story where life begins. The garden is where the Creator God sets the rules of life. In the Adam and Eve garden story, their response to God was basically "Thanks for the advice, but we'll be doing this our way!"[78] Why did Adam and Eve resist God and do their own thing? They wanted to be in control.

I know this feeling well. I want to make suggestions to God on how to make my life work better. I attempt to take control of my life rather than surrender to his thinking and his ways. You see, we were created to be dependent beings—dependent upon our Creator. And if we choose not to be dependent on our Creator, we will inevitably be dependent on something else. It's the problem of who is in control. It's the problem of total surrender!

Aaron, Moses' associate pastor, so to speak, became impatient with Moses for not returning soon enough from his meeting with God. So Aaron gathered everybody's jewelry and melted it down to make a golden calf that would serve as a tangible god for the people.[79] This is a form of control—forming a god you can see, touch, and visit at will.

Throughout history, the agenda of control has been prevalent. Do you think Constantine had any other agenda than control? The Crusades were all about control. The threat of religious persecution operates under the agenda of control. The fear of hell always seems to work best to control the people.

Shortcuts to God are an attractive agenda. Everyone wants to know for sure they have done or are doing what's necessary to receive their ticket to get into heaven. Membership, confirmation, baptism, a clean life, volunteer service, and financial contributions are just a few of the things on the punch card.

In my world it was going forward at an altar call, so at one point I counted about thirty-six times I went to the altar (forty-two, if I count youth camp). But nothing ever changed. Somehow it never made much difference.

Shortcuts become problematic. When you think you have your pass or ticket, you tend to condemn others who didn't come to God in the same way. They just aren't going to make it. They're not one of us, so they are out of luck.

Reformation is the third agenda of the culting process. It feeds on the first two agenda dynamics—control and shortcuts. Reformation's agenda is to change behavior and therefore control these behaviors. Reformation's agenda searches for shortcuts to make the behavioral changes easier.

The problem is that reformation rarely goes far enough. Reformation can only change the outside—fit you into a behavioral mold. Reformation is a little like straightening deck chairs on the *Titanic*. The deck looks better, but the boat is still going to sink. What is desperately needed is *transformation*—from the inside out.

The culting process is alive and well today as it was in the first century. Keep the people under control. Search for the shortcuts that short-circuit the process of life's journey. Find a way to get that ticket into heaven and look on others with pity. Don't seek to be transformed. Seek to get others to reform their ways and come along with the herd—your particular herd is best! The Jewish law had 248 commandments and 365 prohibitions. That's 613 laws to keep! Do you see how easy it would be to pick and choose what's most important to you?

Most every religious system has a similar list—some more, some less. It's no wonder religion has been so divisive throughout history. But what if we determined to major in the majors and minor in the minors? This is Jesus' point throughout his teachings.

Major in the *Person* of God; minor in the *program*.

Major in the *relationship* with God; minor in the *religion*.

The culting process doesn't have a chance if we make the main thing the main thing!

The Opposite of Culting: Transformation

The unhealthy culting process offers only a change on the outside—on the surface. The culting process encourages reformation as the required standard for being truly spiritual. One follows the requirements of doing the "right" things, hanging out with the "right" people, joining the "right" Church or religious institution, believing that doing these "right" things will bring about an acceptable and satisfying spiritual change of the heart. But when you face the major problems of life, all of the acts of reforming your life will not be sufficient. In some ways, it's like an alcoholic who attends the meetings and embraces the lingo but never allows himself to surrender his will and his life to the care and direction of God. He's reformed—a little bit fixed—but he is not changed. He's not transformed.

Maybe the Bible's best illustration of the difference Jesus makes in a person's life through transformation can be viewed in the life of Paul.

Paul had a role in life—to persecute the followers of the Way.[80] The Way believed Jesus was the promised Messiah. Paul was a believer in the Messiah too. He was looking for the Messiah, the Christ. He could have been called a Christian—a follower of the Christ, the Messiah. So, since he wasn't buying into the Messiahship of Jesus, he did all he could do to stop the efforts of the Way—the followers of Jesus. He saw this as his role in life and played it very well. In fact, he felt he was quite righteous about what he was doing. But Jesus apprehended him.

When Jesus comes into your life, he takes you out of your role, or false self, and brings a spirit of authenticity to you and your lifestyle. You can't cover up and play a role when Jesus is leading and you're following him.

Note the words God spoke to Ananias about Paul: "Go, for he is a chosen instrument of Mine, to bear *My name* before the Gentiles and kings and the sons of Israel; for I will show him how much he must suffer for *My* name's sake."[81] This was most important to the Lord—that Paul bear the name of Jesus.

This is what is most important for us today too! We are not commanded to spread Christianity or any other religious system, nor Church membership, but only and primarily to spread the name of Jesus.

The transformation of Saul, the persecutor of the people of Jesus, into Paul, the representer of Jesus, was dramatic and obvious. After spending several days with the disciples of Jesus who were in Damascus, he immediately began to proclaim the name of Jesus in the synagogues. Even more than proclaiming Jesus, Paul was confidently proving that Jesus was the Messiah. The people were shocked![82]

I see the lesson of Paul's encounter with Jesus in this way: when Jesus apprehends you on your way to becoming a righteous Christian, he will transform you into becoming a stubborn follower of him in order to lift up his name. His name is Jesus.

Instead ...

Jesus apprehended my life nearly eight years ago as a seminary graduate and pastor. I had always loved Jesus and taught about him in the ministry opportunities that were laid out for me. But now there is a difference.

These are some of the changes that have happened in my heart and mind:

- Instead of being intent on teaching Scripture properly and effectively, I am more intent on obeying Jesus.
- Instead of doing, doing, doing as well as I can do, I am into being, being, being who Jesus has made me to be.
- Instead of building the Church of Jesus, I am disciplining myself to be the church of Jesus.
- Instead of playing a role or wearing the mask that befits a religious position, I am bent on being real and authentic.
- Instead of trying to reach the masses with another "powerful" message, I am now more interested in investing my time with a few.
- Instead of exercising my life over what "my" purpose is, I am exercising myself toward loving God with all my heart and loving my neighbors as myself.
- Instead of deceiving myself into thinking I have some messianic touch to help people, I introduce them to the only one who can change their lives—Jesus.
- Instead of just going to Church, I am now practicing being the church in every gathering of believers in his name.

- Instead of frantically trying to change the world by Wednesday noon, I now understand that the call of Jesus on my life is a call into his rest.
- Instead of making disciples out of Christians, I see that the best potential disciples are made out of non-Christians.
- Instead of hanging out with the religious crowd, I am hanging out with revolutionaries.
- Instead of doing life as the Lone Ranger, I am now doing life with a few others.
- Instead of counting the variety of Churches in the world, I now see there is only one church—the church of Jesus.
- Instead of doing things my way for Jesus, I am now waiting on Jesus to lead out with his orders and opportunities—to do things his way in his time.

A personal encounter with Jesus will change all that you are and all that you do. That's what happened to Paul. That's what happened to me. And that's what can happen to you too if you'll avoid the temptations of "everything but Jesus" and stick with simply Jesus.

CHAPTER 7

Was Jesus a Christian?

Whether you see Jesus as a great man, a guru, a teacher, a prophet, or a higher power, there is no doubt that he stands in a preeminent position throughout history. Now remember, I'm not talking religion or a religious system. I'm not even speaking about Christianity. I am referring to Jesus alone, *simply* Jesus.

The question I want you to consider is this: Was Jesus a Christian?

My contention is that he wasn't.

To identify Jesus as a Christian is to limit him to the Western culture, to deny his Middle Eastern roots, and to prevent him from being embraced by the rest of the world.

The belief that Jesus was a Christian is a myth, and a deadly one at that. History has proven this over and over. Let's examine a few foundational myths about Jesus and Christianity.

Myth 1: Jesus Is Owned by Christianity

Now, don't get nervous about this. There is nothing wrong with being a Christian or belonging to Christianity. I want to help you consider a very basic understanding that causes lots of misunderstanding both in my native country and in nations around the world.

Most people assert that Jesus was a Christian. Most would agree that Jesus would be comfortable being called a Christian and identifying himself exclusively with Christianity.

But it is a myth. And the collateral damage from this myth has been devastating.

Many Christians believe they have a corner on the market with respect to Jesus. The by-product of believing Jesus is owned by Christianity is an ugly religious pride.

This pride leads Christians to identify their culture as the "right" culture—the "right" way of life. As described in the Hebrew Scriptures, the Jews were the chosen people of God. Today, though, Christians believe that they are the chosen people of God. This belief excludes all other socio-religious communities God created. But Christians have their answer—all others must convert to become Christians!

If you desire to become a follower of Jesus, this misconception will distract you and others away from him. Instead of following Jesus, the focus can so easily shift to becoming a Christian, defending Christianity, and setting out on a mission of converting others to become Christians. All of this distraction leaves Jesus behind.

Most non-Christians believe Jesus is exclusively related to Christians, and therefore they have no possible relationship with him, even though Jesus is so attractive, irresistible, and relevant to them.

Most non-Christians identify Jesus with the disastrous and horrendous events of the Christian past and present. They think of such actions as the Crusades against the Muslims and the persecution and killings of the

Jews—all undertaken in the name of Christianity. The collateral damage is that Jesus becomes guilty by association.

Most non-Christians identify Christianity with the West. And as they develop hate for the West, they develop hate for Christianity (and vice versa). When Christians attempt to convert people who are not Christians, they stir up much anger and hate, especially in the non-Christian cultures. Christians want Hindus, Buddhists, Jews, Muslims, and others to become Christians—to be converted away from their socio-religious community into Western Christianity. This aggressive approach was never the way of Jesus.

Nowhere is this more explosive than within the two opposing narratives between Muslims and Christians. The Muslims don't trust Christians, due to the fear of the Christian missionary attempt to convert them out of their socio-religious community into the Christian socio-religious community. This means tearing them away from their families and cultural traditions. Add any war against the extreme Islamists, and you have tinges of the Crusades.

The Christian narrative is that the Muslims are out to destroy all Christians as infidels. Christians are sending out all kinds of Internet warnings about the worldwide Muslim takeover of the world and attempt to put the world under strict Sharia law. In fact, the claim is that the Muslims will take over the world by birthrate alone. Their numbers are growing much faster than any Christian society.

So the Christian answer to this threat of worldwide domination is basically twofold: First, convert all Muslims to Christianity. Second, nuke the Muslims! Both are absolutely impossible to do, and both are actually attempts to destroy the Muslims. This is nutty thinking!

Three Truths to Debunk the First Myth

The first myth is that Jesus is owned by Christianity. I see three ways to debunk this popular myth:

First, Jesus never used the term "Christian." In fact, only two writers of the Bible ever mentioned it—Luke twice and Peter once.[83] Not only Jesus, but also Matthew, Mark, John, Paul, James, and Jude never mentioned the term so far as we know. So if you must be a Christian to get into heaven, then Matthew, Mark, Paul, James, Jude, Abraham, Isaac, Jacob, and David will not make it!

When I use the argument that Jesus never used the term "Christian," I am saying that he had something much more different in mind than to offer a label to be worn or an organization to join—all to be foisted upon the cultures of the world. If Jesus were trying to change people's cultural identification, he would have actually done so. *But he didn't!*

Not only is the term "Christian" rarely mentioned, but we know it is a man-made term. At first, "Christian" was used as one of the many tags placed on the followers of Jesus. It was never intended as a serious organizational label. "People of the Way" and "Nazarenes" were also popular identifications.[84]

Emperor Constantine chose a group of bishops to meet in AD 325 for the purpose of establishing a creed for the new religion that would be the basis for his political kingdom. He didn't do this for religious reasons; he did it for political reasons. So the bishops settled on the formation of the Christian Church. It was out of this meeting that the early creeds of Christianity were written. This was the official launch of Christianity.

Second, Jesus had a better term. Most Christians love to use the ID "believer" or "born again," yet there seems to be a better designation for those who are into Jesus: a "follower of Jesus," much like the New Testament designation of "followers of the Way." This doesn't negate faith or belief. You must believe enough to be a follower of Jesus. This is Jesus' designation of those who are in relationship with him—*followers.*

Jesus wasn't looking for believers; he was looking for those who believe to follow in his steps. Jesus calls on all to follow him, and he repeatedly uses the term "disciple" and even commands all of his followers to "make disciples of all nations"! A disciple is a learner or a follower. If you call yourself a believer or a born-again Christian, you are not using the clearest, most universally communicative term for those who hear you. Most of the time I say, "I grew up Christian, but I like to call myself a follower of Jesus."

Third, there is nothing wrong with being a Christian, or even a Western Christian, if that's your cultural background. But there is something far better, and that is to be a follower of Jesus. One of the largest spiritual movements in the world is happening among animists in Africa, Buddhists and Hindus in Asia, Muslims and Jews in the Middle East and around the world, atheists and agnostics in China, and even Christians in the United States. This movement numbers in the millions. Other than those within the Western Christian cultural context, this movement consists of people who do not identify themselves with Christianity or Western Christianity, but who sincerely and enthusiastically call themselves followers of Jesus.

People everywhere, no matter their socio-religious community and background, have come to love and even worship Jesus!

How can this be?

Because Jesus is more preeminent than we have let him be. Jesus doesn't fit into any religious box. He is the most attractive, the most irresistible, and the most relevant.

The Jesus Movement

One of the great privileges Diana and I have is to meet and interact with people from most of the socio-religious communities of our world. We have met Muslim leaders—imams, sheiks, corporate, political—who have come to know and love Jesus in a personal way and are now leading other Muslims to do the same.

We have met the leaders who represent millions of Hindus who are meeting in homes to study and worship Jesus. They don't call themselves Christians and don't call their gatherings Churches, but they know and love Jesus. We are intimately aware of Buddhists who are following Jesus—young Buddhists being mentored to follow Jesus, monks, corporate and political leaders who as Buddhists are seriously following Jesus as their Master. We work with several representatives of the more secretive mission operations around the world.

From this vantage point, we are amazed and thrilled to meet people from non-Christian socio-religious communities who love Jesus, pray to Jesus, carefully follow Jesus, and freely share the message of the gospel—Jesus—within their communities.

My friends and I have come together with these same non-Christian lovers of Jesus and shared together what we call a "covenant supper" (Christians know this as Communion), each time experiencing an outflowing of tears throughout the taking of the cup and bread as Jesus did. We share it together as a remembrance of our commitment to Jesus and to one another, until we see Jesus again.

A common experience is for these new followers of Jesus to desire to be baptized—following in the footsteps of Jesus and through baptism outwardly committing to follow Jesus the rest of their lives. I have witnessed this, and it is a thrilling experience!

I've also been amazed that so many of these non-Christian followers of Jesus respond to him in the same way as the early disciples, taking several years to really get it. After following Jesus for perhaps three or four years, they will come to me and share, "Jesus is my Lord. Jesus is my God!" This is coming from their own study of Jesus and the transformational power of Jesus' Spirit in their hearts.

Those of us who work within the Jesus movement in non-Christian socio-religious communities are careful not to share specific locations and names freely in books, articles, and interviews. The reason? There will be some well-meaning Christians who feel the need to get to these people, their leaders, and their groups and attempt to bring them the full and true gospel. This is because they have such difficulty accepting that anyone from another culture could experience Jesus in a different way than they have been taught. These well-meaning Christians want the world to become Christian. They are convinced no one can know Jesus and not be one of them—Christian. This reminds me of the disciples' complaint to Jesus:

> "Master," said John, "we saw someone driving out demons in your name and we tried to stop him, because he is not one of us."
>
> "Do not stop him," Jesus said, "for whoever is not against you is for you."[85]

Myth 2: Jesus Is the Founder of Christianity

This myth may be one of the most difficult for people of all cultures to accept as a myth, but hear me out. Open up your heart and mind and let's examine why I call this a myth. Remember, we're trying to understand the teachings and principles of Jesus, not the teachings and principles of our religious instruction and backgrounds. If I were to hold on to my background understandings, I would still believe Jesus was a Baptist!

Most people throughout the world believe that Jesus founded Christianity and the Christian Church. Earlier I referred to the political act of Constantine that officially established the Christian Church and its creeds. Even though this is a fact, many still assume that Jesus' intent and purpose was to found the religious system of Christianity as God's home on earth and to establish the organized Church as God's way of changing the world.

Jesus did say, "I will build my church."[86] But his idea of the church was an organism, not an institution; a movement, not an establishment; a gathering of followers, not a gathering of creeds, relics, and property. The organized Church provides lots of services for the consumer, but it wasn't what Jesus intended. In Jesus' time there already was an organized Church in existence—the synagogue. He didn't speak against it, but only against its leadership.

The synagogue of Jesus' time and the organized Church today are very similar in their structure and functionality. They are both local gathering places for larger-than-home-sized events. They meet regularly. They both are more for the spectator than for the participant. No matter how hard the organized Church works to promote small groups in homes, the primary meeting is the weekly gathering, and the Church is equated with that meeting.

I believe Jesus came to make disciples in all the nations. This is best accomplished through small, participatory groups. These dynamic gatherings quickly become viral. When the big-C Church of China was forbidden to meet in China and the missionaries were thrown out, the little-c church, or gathering of Jesus followers, multiplied. The organization became an organism—a Jesus movement that couldn't be stopped!

There are many big-C Churches that have dismantled the organizational structure that tied them to a building and are transforming into more of a movement. (I'm not suggesting this is the way to go, because I still see the value of the synagogue-like function of the Church in a community.) Friends of mine in Texas have shifted their sizable Church into a meeting once a month on Saturday evening of all of the followers of Jesus in their community. Weekly they meet in homes on Sunday mornings, Saturday evenings, whenever the smaller core fellowships decide to gather. There is no doubt where the power and center of this Church is. It's in the active participation of their people in the smaller core groups. Then monthly they all come together to share what's going on in their groups and in their lives.

The big-C Church as the focus of attention is not what Jesus had in mind. And the damage of believing the myth that Jesus founded Christianity or the organized Christian Church is threefold.

The religion of Christianity and the organized Church tends to become a substitute for a personal relationship with Jesus and his people. Jesus commonly is left out of the Christian, religious expression of faith.

The experience of the organized Church tends to create spectators and not participants. It's just too easy to check off Church attendance as one of the things you feel you must do. But as powerful as the Church experience might be through authentic worship and exceptional messages, the once-a-week "show" just isn't what Jesus intended. The Jews already had this experience in the synagogue. There's nothing wrong with it. But Jesus had a better idea!

When you believe Jesus is the founder of Christianity or of the organized Christian Church, you expect him to be the architect of what is done in the name of Christianity and by the local organized Christian Church. The result of this thinking? Jesus gets the blame for whatever goes wrong. He gets tied to the moral failures of pastors. He gets tied to the endless fundraisers, the misappropriation of funds, the lavish lifestyles, the excessive expenditures.

Jesus *was* a founder. But not of the Church as we know it. And not of Christianity as we know it.

To link Jesus with the organized Church or with the religious system of Christianity caricatures Jesus beyond recognition. The world then criticizes Jesus and his movement on earth based upon the attitudes and actions of the Church and the religious system.

The Beauty of the Little-c Church

To believe the second myth limits Jesus in almost every way. He is pre-eminent above all things, peoples, and religious systems. To put Jesus in the position of founder of Christianity keeps him in an exclusive box, unavailable to the rest of the world.

Neither Jesus nor his disciples bashed the synagogue of their day, which equates to the Church today. There was no movement to plant new synagogues (Churches) to compete with the primary synagogue in the city.

The mission that Paul and others were on was to make disciples of Jesus in all nations (cultures). As Jesus was introduced into a socio-religious community, people who responded were urged to walk together—to follow Jesus together—in the spirit of what we read in Acts 2:42–47. They gathered together to study the teachings of Jesus, pray together, eat together, and fellowship together. These little gatherings naturally took place primarily in homes. There was no thought of building buildings. Those buildings were already in place in the synagogues and were not needed for the Jesus movement to thrive.

Therefore, the dynamic, relational movement Jesus launched was not about building an organization or a monument; he set in motion a movement that was loosely held together. This movement was not to take the place of the synagogue, nor is it to take the place of the organized (big-*C*) Church today. The Jesus movement takes precedence over any organization or religious system.

It was to be a movement that orbited around and within the synagogue (Church), the community, and the marketplace, demonstrating the love of Jesus to all. This movement doesn't have the motive of gathering spectators together, because it's all about participation in a fellowship, learning to love God and love one another. I call this movement the church of Jesus with a little *c*—the gathering of the followers of Jesus into a fellowship. It's a place to learn how to share, live life, and practice the principles and teachings of Jesus.

Big-*C* Church was not taught, nor was it in his mind or in the practice of the early disciples as they spread the message of Jesus and the Kingdom. In fact, the term "church" was not a major one for Jesus. Jesus uses the term "church" only three times, because his primary teaching was the good news of the Kingdom.[87]

The purpose of the movement is to do one of the most difficult things ever—introduce Jesus to the world by demonstrating him to the world, by walking, talking, thinking, and loving like Jesus. You see, Jesus doesn't want you to demonstrate *for* him, but to be a demonstration *of* him—of his love and his peace.

Jesus launched a revolutionary movement. Are you participating in this movement—the orbiting (little-c) church movement Jesus founded—or are you still a spectator in a big-C Church? You can do both and gain much out of your experience, but don't miss out on making the Jesus movement your priority right where you live. Jesus is already moving in the world around you. He's looking for you to join him there.

One couple with whom we walk with Jesus have set up a study/fellowship evening at their home every Tuesday night. They have become convinced the most important aspect of this little gathering is that they are consistently there, no matter what, every Tuesday night. People come and go, but they know this home is open and welcoming to them on any Tuesday night. There's something refreshing in our world about consistency.

Another couple has spent their time and energy following Jesus' commandment of loving your neighbor as yourself. They have taken this neighborhood love to a whole new level. They don't preach to their neighbors. They don't invite them to a Church. They don't get caught up in the divisive gossip of the neighborhood. They do something entirely different. They have determined to be Jesus to their neighbors—live, think, love, listen, and talk like Jesus to their neighbors.

They have become loving neighbors in their community, and the members of this community are responding in positive ways. They listen to problems and concerns. They laugh with their neighbors and cry with them. In some ways, according to a Jesus standard, they act normally in their neighborhood with a lot of authentic, nonjudgmental love. We desperately need more "normal" neighbors, living life in the love of Jesus. This is what the Jesus movement is to be about. This is Kingdom living at its best!

The Jesus movement that orbits around the organized Church and the community is not made up only of Christians. The Jesus movement includes a vast variety of people from all kinds of cultural backgrounds. What holds this movement together is that each person, no matter his or her religious background, is a follower of Jesus.

Myth 3: Jesus Is Narrow and Exclusive

In Jesus' first seminar in Matthew 5–7, he made a radical statement with respect to his relationship with the Jewish Law and the Prophets. He said, "Do not think that I have come to abolish the Law or the Prophets; I have not come to abolish them but to fulfill them."[88]

The Jewish culture, with its Law and traditions, was like a glass container, so to speak. Jesus came to fill that glass to the brim. He came to bring ultimate meaning and fullness to the Jewish religious system. Jesus is the way, the truth, and the life for all the Jewish dreams and yearnings. In the same way, I believe that he is the way, the truth, and the life for all cultural and religious systems and traditions. He is the meaning and fullness everyone is looking for. He fills up the various glasses of every culture.

This may seem a little far-fetched to you at first, but give it some thought. We are finding the footprints of Jesus in every culture. Years ago, Don Richardson wrote a groundbreaking book, *Eternity in Their Hearts*.[89] He demonstrated that the fingerprints of the Creator God were found in many cultures. God is already there, because God placed "eternity in their hearts."

Similarly, the movie *Fingerprints of God* in Japan clearly reveals the Creator God of the Japanese people. In the past (and this is still happening today in some places) the Japanese people were told they had to reject their Japanese roots and culture in order to be converted to Western Christianity. However, it is now clear that the Creator God of the Japanese people was known to be in the form of a tri-unity, or Godhead. Their Creator God had a Japanese name, Ameno-mi-nakanushi, not the Jewish name, Jehovah. When the Japanese watch this film, they weep with joy. They don't have to reject their culture or feel they are an afterthought of God; God created them and is already present there.

This same understanding has happened among the Hawaiians and Polynesians, Buddhists, Hindus, and Chinese. What's interesting is that in many of these cultures there are similar stories—the flood, sacrifices for sins, and a garden scene. In several of these cultures, their ancient scriptures speak of a sacrifice for their sins that must be made by God himself.

Where did these stories come from?

These are the fingerprints of God in the many cultures of the world.

Anyone in any culture or on any continent can be a follower of Jesus—cultural Jews, Hindus, Buddhists, animists, agnostics, Muslims, and Christians can all be followers of Jesus. Christians have said for years that a cultural Jew doesn't have to renounce being Jewish in order to follow Jesus. Following Jesus can make a person's Jewishness more full and meaningful. I believe this translates into the many cultures of the world in the same way. A cultural Buddhist can be a follower of Jesus. A cultural Muslim can be a follower of Jesus. It's just like a cultural Catholic can be a follower of Jesus without renouncing his cultural background, or a cultural Baptist or a cultural Methodist. Anyone can be a follower of Jesus and still remain within his or her cultural background. Jesus demonstrated this with every encounter.

Christianity isn't the way, the truth, and the life.

The Church isn't the way, the truth, and the life.

Jesus is!

CHAPTER 8

Jesus Trumps Everything!

At the Dalai Lama event where I spoke in San Francisco, Diana sat next to a man who has worked closely with His Holiness, especially in helping his people who live in and out of Tibet. This man embraces the Buddhist way of life and has been highly successful in his business ventures over the years. Diana didn't tell him that her husband was one of the speakers on the platform. (I think she needed an out in case I wasn't received well.)

As I noted before, I was the last to be introduced. When it was clear to her that I was being warmly received, especially by her new friend, she whispered, "That's my husband." As soon as I finished and the gathering was dismissed, he made his way up to me. He said, "I've never heard about Jesus in this way ever in my life! I love it! I think, to sum up your remarks, I would say, 'Jesus trumps everything!'"

I wholeheartedly agreed.

But is that right? Does Jesus trump *everything*?

Let's take a look at four crucial areas and see for ourselves.

1. Jesus Came to Restore What the Human Race Has Lost

Jesus restores humankind to Eden.

In the well-known Garden of Eden story, Adam and Eve enjoyed the presence of God. They were all set—good jobs, lush place to live, great retirement benefits, and a personal relationship with God.

They were to fulfill three purposes:

- Together they were to reflect the image of the Creator God.
- They were to reproduce that image by filling the earth with children.
- They were to reign together against evil to cultivate and guard the garden as co-rulers with God.

Both Eve and Adam made a fatal mistake, not only in failing God, but also in failing each other. They had only one prohibition that was set up by God. However one wants to characterize that prohibition and the subsequent encounter with the serpent that lured them into breaking the universal law set up by their Creator, *they blew it!* They blew it by not trusting their Creator God and by disobeying what he said.

What's interesting is that, by disobeying him, not only did they break the law but also the law broke them. They were expelled from the Garden with three consequences:

- They lost the Kingdom where they were co-rulers with their Creator.
- They lost the personal relationship with the Creator God.
- They lost the abiding presence of God's Spirit.

Ever since those losses, humankind has been desperately trying to recover. Every religion, philosophy, and political ideology is an attempt to fill that hole in the soul, where there is a deep yearning for fulfillment and joy. Each is an attempt to seek the Kingdom that was lost in the

Garden, to seek to reestablish a personal relationship with the Creator, and to seek to restore the abiding presence of God.

Most every religion sets up a system (and often an obstacle course to make your way through) in order to get out of this painful place and get to Heaven, Nirvana, Eden, Shangri-la, Paradise, or the Promised Land. Every religious system is a well-meaning attempt with its own desires and standards. Christians are trying to be the best Christians, Buddhists the best Buddhists, and so on with Hindus, Muslims, Jews, and animists. Since God created all peoples and is holding them together, eternity has been placed in everyone's heart. This is why people worldwide search for God. At the core of the search is this deep ache from the hole in the soul. Everyone is seeking the Kingdom, seeking that personal relationship with the Creator God, and seeking an abiding presence with God as in the beginning in the Garden of Eden.

But setting up ways to get out of here isn't the way of God; it's the way of humankind. Nor is it God's way to set up a system of dos and don'ts to avoid going to hell. It's interesting to note that there was no system set up in the Garden of Eden and no worship, but only a relationship with the Creator God, walking together in the Garden. This is why, after establishing a massive system of sacrifices and feasts, God says through the prophets, "I want compassion rather than your sacrifices."[90] God wants a relationship. There is a simple distinction made between religion and relationship. Religion is humanity's best attempt to avoid going to hell. Relationship says, "I've already been to hell and don't want to go back!"

Religion is our idea.

Relationship is God's idea.

After being taught and teaching otherwise, I've come to the conclusion that God never intends to take those who respond to him out of here. Even with Jesus' teachings about his return and the end of the world, he has not given us a way to get out of here. That's not the direction! God is doing all he can to get down here—to dwell among us. So this is what God has been up to ever since the human race lost the Kingdom, the personal relationship, and the abiding presence of God. Through the priests, the judges, the kings, and the prophets, God wanted to dwell among those who would trust him, and those people would be a blessing to all the nations of the world.

After the prophets, there was a period of four hundred silent years. It was at this point that Jesus was sent to earth. His mission was to reveal the good news of the Kingdom and, by doing this, to restore what humankind had lost. Jesus repeatedly announced the Kingdom, he established the personal relationship, and he introduced the abiding presence of God for all to experience.

Jesus brought the Kingdom of God to earth, because he is the King. Wherever the King is, there is the Kingdom. He was the dwelling place of God on earth, fully indwelt with the Spirit of God. God had finally come down here to dwell among those who would trust him.

Jesus did one more amazing thing. He reintroduced the Spirit of God as the abiding presence of God—to permanently indwell people again as in the Garden. With this introduction, it is again possible to enjoy a personal relationship with the Creator God—to walk with him in the Garden. So the Kingdom, the personal relationship with God, and his abiding presence are no longer things hoped for, but they have become a reality in Jesus. They're not enjoyed in a lush garden any longer. They are experienced right here, right now—an inner peace in the context of broken pieces.

He came to turn religious stress into rest. Jesus said, "Come to me, all you who are weary and burdened, and I will give you rest. Take my yoke upon you and learn from me, for I am gentle and humble in heart, and you will find rest for your souls. For my yoke is easy and my burden is light."[91] You can have all that was ever lost in the Garden. Jesus can fill up the hole in your soul. Jesus can restore what humankind has lost. It's all about restoration and transformation. And you can never acquire restoration and transformation on your own.

2. Jesus Came to Give You What You Can't Get on Your Own

What is it that Jesus can give you that you can't get on your own?

My entire professional life, I have worked with people at the level of their deepest needs. I jokingly say, "I've counseled half of Orange County since 1975, and I feel like the other half is coming in this month." When you grapple with people's problems, it doesn't take long to see what they are.

For too long I believed I had the answers to their needs and struggles. I didn't! The bottom line is, I could only suggest some tools for them to help themselves. But these tools, good as they might be, at best only enable people to achieve a level of self-reformation. Certainly this is helpful, but reformation can only work with symptoms—the external manifestation. What is needed is transformation at the core level—an inner change of heart.

Since I've been following Jesus, I have found the difference he makes in four emotional situations has become amazingly real to me. On the negative side of the emotional ledger, we humans are continually struggling with fear, anger, guilt, and shame. Jesus offers a positive counter-experience to each of these toxic emotions:

- peace that counteracts the fear
- love that counteracts the anger
- joy that counteracts the guilt
- grace that counteracts the shame

And what is even more amazing is that I and the others I am walking with are hearing that those who are fighting the toughest battles are also experiencing the difference a relationship with Jesus makes. They are fighting the experiences of betrayal, divorce, and death of a loved one. They are fighting the ongoing treatment of cancer, international peace negotiations, and financial disasters. They are fighting in the military and seeing families torn apart. They are surviving the wearisome conflicts of others, along with a variety of addictions.

What is really needed is a genuine change of heart—to see your life, predicaments, and people differently. Several years ago, we set out to study only the five Gospels for three years—Matthew, Mark, Luke, John, and Acts. We did this in order to get to know this Jesus. That focus proved to be life changing!

It was through our Jesus journey that we discovered what only Jesus could do for us. I have no capability to change a person's heart. I can't give people peace. I can't give people joy. I can't give them love. I can't . . . but I've come to realize that Jesus can!

Again, I am not speaking of the religious Jesus. I am referring to the most prominent and powerful Person ever. And, in the most pragmatic way, this Jesus seems to be able to effect these internal changes in people. Even though I have experienced this personally and have observed repeatedly his effect in people who need what he has, I still find myself caught up in the joy of actually seeing it happen.

There's something about Jesus without religious baggage—his words, his actions, his loving ways, his bent toward the disenfranchised, and especially his name—that brings healing and wholeness to the heart and mind. Jesus is truly the most effective Person you can embrace for yourself.

Experiences in Jesus

Here are four of the life-transforming experiences our little core group of followers is finding in Jesus:

The experience of peace. Jesus was all about peace. Peace is not just the absence of conflict or a cessation of the battles waging in us and around us. It's a sense of inner calm that everything is going to be all right.

When Jesus first sent his disciples out, he told them to go into villages and give the blessing of peace to those who were interested.[92] Frequently, Jesus said to troubled people, "Go in peace."[93]

At the last gathering of Jesus' disciples before his death, he said, "Peace I leave with you; My peace I give to you; not as the world gives do I give to you. Do not let your heart be troubled, nor let it be fearful."[94] And later in that gathering he said, "These things I have spoken to you, so that in Me you may have peace."[95]

After his death and resurrection, Jesus appeared to his disciples and set them up for a special mission. Jesus said, "Peace be with you! As the Father has sent me, I am sending you."[96] As soon as Jesus said this, he empowered them to go into the world and bring peace to everyone they met. Jesus brought peace to everyone he met. Now he is sending out all of his followers to do the same—to be peacemakers, agents of reconciliation, wherever they go.

One of our closest friends, someone with whom we have been doing life together for many years, was struck with a rare form of cancer. In his battle Jeff endured a variety of chemo and radiation treatments and struggled with the depressing results of his fight. He was a most knowledgeable patient and was known as a fighter in every way. Jeff tried his best to find peace through many channels. But he was losing his sense of peace while walking through this horrendous struggle.

When Jeff shared his depression with our little core group, I confessed that I had no additional answers for him but that I knew Jesus did. We had prayed for, with, and over Jeff on several occasions over the course of a few years. His desperation, though, required something more than our prayers. I moved into gear with my new thinking of sending him to ask for that peace from Jesus himself.

A couple of days later Jeff was sitting in his favorite chair in his home. He was all alone, and in his feelings of desperation and depression, he cried out to Jesus for help. He affirmed that he believed Jesus was the only way out of this death struggle and asked for one thing—peace.

Later he shared with the group that he felt a hand on his shoulder. He felt an indescribable presence that was reassuring to him, and a most amazing sense of peace came over him. He knew everything was going to be okay.

As he shared his story with us, we were all feeling the peace that only Jesus can give. We all knew through one of our closest brothers that this Jesus we follow together is so real and so wonderful! We weren't reading about it; we were experiencing it firsthand!

Although we lost Jeff a few months ago, his experience, strength, and peace in Jesus still speak to us as we gather together. We are all aware of it!

Through Jesus, peace is available to anyone who wants it. This is the kind of peace that you just can't get on your own.

The experience of joy. Joy is different from happiness. Happiness depends upon the happenings that are going on right now. Joy is an inner quality of seeing things with a positive perspective. Joy is the ability to enjoy the scenery when you are on a detour!

When Jesus was born, it was announced that he was to be the good news of great joy for all people.[97] Much later, at a special final gathering with his disciples, Jesus said, "These things I have spoken to you so that My joy may be in you, and that your joy may be made full."[98] Jesus was teaching them about their relationship with him, that it is as vital as a branch connected to the vine. As a follower remains connected to Jesus, he or she will experience the same joy Jesus possessed. Think of it. You can have Jesus' joy in you in all its brimming fullness, spilling over into every area of your life and into the lives of others!

Diana and I have the privilege of working with hundreds of people locally and many more around the world. It's a wonderful privilege, yet it's full of exhausting, long hours of counseling, conversation, parties, breakfasts, lunches, dinners, and a never-ending series of coffee meetings day in and day out. We committed a long time ago to stop initiating unnecessary meetings that can drain our energy. Instead we began a habit of waiting on Jesus to bring people to us and to give us the wisdom and energy to handle this flow of people.

We are both only children and both are introverts at our core. This new commitment to wait on Jesus to send people our way was a big one to us—an unnatural one. When we get tired, we can lose our joy in the process of doing what we do. Although we have asked Jesus to send us people who need a touch from him, we have felt at times like praying for Jesus to slow the flow of people down a bit. We now have found that when we are feeling exhaustion coming on and Jesus sends another person our way, or another dinner, or another gathering to attend, Jesus comes through in a big way with a major shot of spiritual adrenaline to receive this new person or event as from him. And at the end of the encounter, we both marvel at how empowered and encouraged we are by these "interruptions" in our lives. There is no greater joy than to be personal channels of the touch of Jesus.

Jesus challenged his followers by saying, "Until now you have asked for nothing in My name; ask and you will receive, so that your joy may be made full."[99] And as Jesus prayed, he said, "But now I come to You; and these things I speak in the world so that they may have My joy made full in themselves."[100]

Do you get the picture that Jesus is bent on his followers experiencing joy? Through Jesus, joy is available to anyone who wants it.

The experience of love. Although peace and joy are commonly identified with Jesus, love is the primary theme of who Jesus is and what he taught. Most Christian children know the song "Jesus Loves Me." Jesus is the epitome of love. To act like Jesus is to do the loving thing.

Jesus taught that his followers ought to learn to love God. He said, "You shall love the Lord your God with all your heart, and with all your soul, and with all your mind."[101] This concept provides a centering effect in your life.

There's something fundamental about loving someone greater than yourself—something of an inner balance that keeps you and your life in proper perspective.

Along with loving God, Jesus taught his followers, "You shall love your neighbor as yourself."[102] Jesus' teaching on loving your neighbor requires you to love anyone in need. Jesus said there is no commandment greater than these two.[103]

Jesus went further in his teachings on love by instructing his followers to love one another, whether they were in need of anything or not. He said to his disciples, "A new commandment I give to you, that you love one another, even as I have loved you, that you also love one another. By this all men will know that you are My disciples, if you have love for one another."[104] To Jesus, this experience of love is not just to love God and to love your neighbor but to *love one another.* Loving one another is to be the mark of one who is a follower of Jesus.

Next, Jesus extended this love theme to include enemies. You want to know how to eliminate your enemies? Love them! Jesus said, "I say to you who hear, love your enemies, do good to those who hate you. . . . If you love those who love you, what credit is that to you? For even sinners love those who love them. . . . But love your enemies, and do good, and lend, expecting nothing in return; and your reward will be great, and you will be sons of the Most High; for He Himself is kind to ungrateful and evil men."[105]

Jesus-style love ranges from loving God, loving your neighbor, loving one another, to the extreme of loving your enemies. What's most convicting to me is that this experience of love is not just an emotional state of being. It's a state of doing, whether you feel it or not.

As I said before, we don't need more love; we need more lovers!

Jesus views our commitment to follow him within a loving relationship. "Just as the Father has loved Me, I have also loved you; abide in My love. If you keep My commandments, you will abide in My love; just as I have kept My Father's commandments and abide in His love. . . . This is My commandment, that you love one another, just as I have loved you."[106] Keeping his commandments means walking in his steps—following his example and teachings.

This love relationship is so tight that a follower of Jesus can actually own the love of God in himself or herself. Jesus said to the Father, "The glory which You have given Me I have given to them, that they may be one, just as We are one; I in them and You in Me, that they [my followers] may be perfected in unity, so that the world may know that You sent Me, and loved them, even as You have loved Me. . . . So that the love with which you loved Me may be in them, and I in them."[107]

Wow! I read these teachings of Jesus and wonder what went wrong. Jesus wants all of his followers to live in unity—to be one—and to love one another. Yet, for the most part, we are divided. And worse, we are proud of it.

Right after the terrorist attack of 9/11, we became activated into fighting the battle against the enemy of our country. We knew the enemy was not all of Islam but the Islamists—the extremists. However, we moved into high gear with our energy and resources and took a strong stand in fighting terrorism. In the process my love for the Jewish people and my prejudice against the Muslim people was triggered. I didn't love the Muslim people, didn't even like them, and at my core I was afraid of them.

It was after this experience that Jesus apprehended my heart and mind, and this caused me to rethink everything I had ever taught or believed. As I was examining my heart early one morning, I came to the realization that I had fear and anger in my heart against Muslims, Arabs, and Palestinians. What bugged me about this realization was that it was suddenly simple to see how wrong I was. All of my arguments against them fell apart in the presence of Jesus. I saw clearly that I couldn't be a follower of Jesus and be on anyone's side.

According to Jesus, I must love everyone. If I couldn't categorize the Muslims as my neighbors, then according to Jesus, I still had to love them as my enemies. There was no wiggle room. I figured I would have to learn to love them.

Well, guess what? I didn't have to *learn* to love Muslims, Arabs, and Palestinians. Jesus *infused me* with the love I needed. Suddenly it wasn't tough to love them.

Let me tell you, what's tough is to stubbornly follow Jesus. Jesus brings the love along! But following him is still the toughest thing I've ever set out to do.

Today we have the most wonderful and loving relationships with so many Muslims, Arabs, and Palestinians. We walk with several Muslims, Arabs, and Palestinians every week. Only Jesus can bring about this kind of love!

The experience of grace. Karma (which is another way of saying that we reap what we sow) is a reality. There are always consequences for our actions. But there is something that trumps karma—grace. Grace is something you don't deserve, something you didn't work for, something you weren't able to plan for or to orchestrate. Grace is given by Jesus, many times with no rhyme or reason to it.

Grace is one of Jesus' primary themes as he touches the untouchable lepers and the unclean, as he opens the eyes of the blind, as he has compassion on the poor and the disenfranchised, as he receives those who are on the outside of the religious world, as he welcomes women and children (those normally pushed aside), and as he chooses the ordinary and uneducated to be the leaders of his movement. Just as grace trumps karma, so does Jesus, the deliverer of grace, trump everything!

Two of the dynamics within the experience of grace are forgiveness and freedom. It's hard to imagine two more powerful life principles than these. And these two dynamics are in tandem with one another.

Every time I bring up the subject of forgiveness, people immediately wake up and take note.

So many are locked up in a state of unforgiveness. Either they long to be forgiven for something they have done or neglected to do, or they are imprisoned by not being willing to forgive someone who has hurt them. Either way, people are stuck in unforgiveness.

When you forgive another person, you set a prisoner free. That prisoner is *you*. Once you experience forgiveness, either by forgiving or being forgiven, you enter into a wonderful sense of freedom.

Several of the most popular radio therapists don't even have forgiveness in their repertoire. This is why, when it comes to really setting people free, they can only do the equivalent of putting bandages on compound fractures.

Forgiveness and freedom are two of Jesus' most powerful principles. Paul, an early follower of Jesus, spoke in a synagogue in Asia Minor to God-fearing Jews and non-Jews as a guest speaker. He said, "I want you to know two things: through Jesus is forgiveness and through Jesus is the kind of freedom the Law of Moses couldn't provide."[108]

Through Jesus, grace is available to anyone who wants it. This is the kind of grace that you just can't get on your own.

All kinds of religious systems and programs offer you lots of things, but Jesus can give you true and lasting peace, joy, love, and grace.

3. Jesus Came to Personalize the God of Gods

Do you remember the story I told earlier in which C. S. Lewis spoke of God writing himself into the play of life through the character of Jesus?[109] The third observation of how Jesus trumps everything is to look at how he played out this character.

Have you ever tried to follow God? Not easy, is it? God seems so out there, so unknowable, and we're not able to understand God completely due to our human limitations. How is it possible to be godly in our lifestyles?

Jesus came to personalize the God of the universe. Jesus came to introduce humankind to him. Jesus came to clarify this God. Jesus invites any who will to follow and get to know this God. It's like Jesus is the point Person—the way to know this God.

Paul wrote a letter to the followers of Jesus in Colossae and made a case for Jesus embodying all of the fullness of God:

> He was supreme in the beginning and—leading the resurrection parade—he is supreme in the end. From beginning to end he's there, towering far above everything, everyone. So spacious is he, so roomy, that everything of God finds its proper place in him without crowding. Not only that, but all the broken and dislocated pieces of the universe—people and

things, animals and atoms—get properly fixed and fit together in vibrant harmonies.[110]

Paul continued, "Everything of God gets expressed in him, so you can see and hear him clearly. You don't need a telescope, a microscope, or a horoscope to realize the fullness of Christ, and the emptiness of the universe without him. When you come to him, that fullness comes together for you, too. His power extends over everything."[111]

All of the fullness of God dwells in Jesus in bodily form. It's all in Jesus! Jesus is the point of it all! Jesus is God fleshed out! Jesus is the visible form we can follow in order to know the invisible God of gods.

In the opening chapter of the Gospel of John, this follower wrote about Jesus, "No one has ever seen God, but the one and only Son, who is himself God and is in closest relationship with the Father, has made him known."[112]

Not even the written Word is equal to Jesus. Jesus stated this clearly to the religious leaders when he said, "You study the Scriptures diligently because you think that in them you have eternal life. These are the very Scriptures that testify about me, yet you refuse to come to me to have life."[113]

The significance of abiding in Jesus is a powerfully insightful teaching that we'll consider in greater length later. But it's important to list it here. Jesus said:

I am the true vine, and my Father is the gardener. He cuts off every branch in me that bears no fruit, while every branch that does bear fruit he prunes so that it will be even more fruitful. . . . Remain in me, as I also remain in you. No branch can bear fruit by itself; it must remain in the vine. Neither can you bear fruit unless you remain in me.

I am the vine; you are the branches. If you remain in me and I in you, you will bear much fruit; apart from me you can do nothing.[114]

This all happens in the name of Jesus with nothing added. Not Miracle-Gro on the leaves. Not mulch on the roots. Just Jesus. Note that it's not without the Spirit you can do nothing, but without *Jesus* you can do nothing.

Check out what Jesus says of the Spirit and the Father here: "I have much more to say to you, more than you can now bear. But when he, the Spirit of truth, comes, he will guide you into all the truth. He will not speak on his own; he will speak only what he hears, and he will tell you what is yet to come. He will glorify me, because it is from me that he will receive what he will make known to you. All that belongs to the Father is mine. That is why I said the Spirit will receive from me what he will make known to you."[115]

Do you see the preeminence of Jesus acted out in the play?

He is the marquee character. The spotlight is always on him.

4. Jesus Dissolves Alienation at Every Level

About eight years ago, when Jesus claimed my wife's heart and my heart in a fresh way, we were struggling with how to say what we do. I had resigned as a pastor and drastically curtailed my speaking engagements in order to authentically walk with Jesus and to walk with others on this spiritual journey. So at this juncture I struggled with what I would say when someone asks, "What do you do?"

I had just left a long luncheon in Arlington, Virginia, where a few men going in the same direction shared with me the kinds of answers they gave when asked that question. The one angle I latched on to was this: "I work with the problem of alienation." I don't know why, but that seemed an attractive handle to me.

When I checked out of the hotel, I asked a woman at the front desk to call me a taxi. She suggested that I take a town car instead for the same price. When the car arrived, the driver was a large man from Cameroon; his name was Joseph Nkodo.

On our way he asked, "What do you do?"

"I work with the problem of alienation."

I thought this would bring any conversation to a halt.

"Oh, alienation," he said, "like between countries and families and villages. How do you work with alienation? What can you do?"

"Well, we don't approach it politically, educationally, or religiously. We have found that the best answers to the problem of alienation are the teachings and principles of Jesus." I found it difficult to get the name of Jesus out of my mouth. It was the weirdest, yet most wonderful, thing. I'd never just presented Jesus to a person.

Joseph didn't skip a beat. "Oh, Jesus. You know, in my country you grow up either Muslim or Catholic. However, it really doesn't matter, because everyone worships their ancestors anyway. But I've always thought Jesus was so different from everything else." Joseph from Cameroon taught me how to speak about Jesus. Joseph and his family have become good friends of ours and they know what it means to follow Jesus.

Since that initiation experience, I've spoken with others about alienation quite often. More often, though, I find myself just sharing illustrations of Jesus dissolving the problem of alienation here and now. Here are several that come to mind:

Jesus trumps competition between denominations and religions. A variety of Church cultures are part of the Christian community. Jesus prayed for all followers to be one in his love, yet Christians tend to be divisive, competitive, and condemning. This causes alienation.

How sad that Christians are so fragmented. My own narrow Baptist roots were so fragmented that we didn't even accept other Baptists. When it came to Catholics, we felt we had nothing to discuss with them. Early on, when I was beginning to embrace Jesus as simply enough, the Catholic Diocese of Orange County invited me to conduct a three-hour training session on how to reach disenchanted Catholics. What an opportunity this was to share the simplicity of following Jesus! We do have so much in common, if we keep the main thing the main thing. Which is Jesus. Simply Jesus.

This oneness for which Jesus prayed goes beyond Western Christian culture.

We are brothers and sisters with all those who are followers of Jesus, whether they are Mormon, Jehovah's Witness, Buddhist, Adventist, Hindu, Baptist, Church of Christ, Jew, Muslim, or whatever.

I wish I had a dollar for every time someone asked me to help him or her understand some other religious system. What they are really asking is, "What are the differences, and how can I argue my beliefs over theirs?" Instead, we must find a common ground of unity in Jesus. There is no barrier between any two of us, no matter who we are, if we are both discussing Jesus. The Jesus movement includes all whom God is calling to himself from every culture.

Jesus trumps the animosity between political parties. One of our privileges is to be able to participate in the President's National Prayer Breakfast each year. Numerous US politicians and representatives from around 160 nations come and gather in the name of Jesus to pray. Political alienation and fighting is all we hear about in the daily news, yet we rarely hear of the many from both the political right and left who have discovered unity in Jesus. So many of these congressmen and senators have carved out a close family friendship through coming together and learning to follow Jesus as the one who matters most in their lives. Their love for one another is a beautiful thing to watch!

Jesus trumps prejudicial conflict. A few years ago, we had a local judge who was brought up on charges of having child porn on his computer. It was a major scandal in the media for quite some time. Los Angeles radio stations sponsored demonstrations from his front yard. It was ugly.

When the judge and I met together, I suggested that he couldn't go through this alienation from others alone. I invited him to come to a weekly study at our training center. We had about one hundred women and fifty men who were going through this particular study. Since he was under house arrest and wore a security anklet, he had to get permission to attend.

The night he showed up, I purposely placed him at a table where my best friend was the table leader and sat him in between a former Irvine police detective, whose primary area of investigation was pornography, and an opinionated former Marine, who preferred to shoot first, then ask questions. No one, except my best buddy, knew this was the judge in the news. As these men around the table finally realized who was at their table, the love and unifying dynamic of Jesus overwhelmed them. They found the power through Jesus to embrace the judge as a brother.

Jesus trumps marital differences. Dear friends of mine have a wonderful story about how Jesus can change a marriage. The husband is a Muslim and his wife is a Catholic. They fell so deeply in love that they didn't count the cost of any religious consequences in the marriage later, especially when children came along.

Their marriage was filled with sniping and bickering, causing serious alienation over their religious and cultural differences. To put it mildly, they were not enjoying their marriage; at best, they were enduring it. They met a friend of mine and shared with him the marital struggles they were experiencing, and he gave them a solution that has worked marvelously over the years. He said, "Why don't you both start following Jesus and unify yourselves around your relationship with him?" Well, they did, and the transformation has been dramatic!

I was just with them last week and they are doing well. They have raised two beautiful young women, and both husband and wife are successful in their vocational endeavors. The secret? Jesus trumped their differences! Both are equally devoted to following Jesus. The common denominator of their marriage is Jesus!

Jesus trumps natural enemies. Recently, Diana and I met two women who were bitter enemies by no fault of their own. You see, one woman's son murdered the son of the other. Both women loved God, yet here they were, both with broken hearts without any way out of this cycle of pain. They had never spoken to each other before. Then, one day in the hallways of a courthouse, they saw one another, stopped, and sobbed in each other's arms. Jesus has now knit their hearts together as the dearest of friends, and they are ministering to others who find themselves in similar situations.

Jesus trumps the alienation you are experiencing personally. Who are you alienated from?

- From yourself?
- From God?
- From your spouse?
- From your children?
- From your parents?
- From your friends?
- From your neighbors?
- From your colleagues?
- From your enemies?

As is the case with most of our personal problems, the bottom-line solution to alienation comes down to one thing—*surrender*. But surrender to what or to whom? Surrender doesn't work in vague terms. Some say, for example, that you must surrender to the "universe," but surrender works best when you can identify where to submit your alienation. And we have found it best to surrender your will and your life to Jesus.

Diana and I know a man who was recently struggling with life and death issues in a psych ward at a local hospital. He asked to be restrained so that he couldn't hurt himself or others. He knew he had to give up the anxiety but didn't know how. His wife suggested that he surrender to Jesus. He did and found the first extended period of rest he'd had in several days.

Jesus can bridge every form of alienation you are experiencing. He alone brings unity, peace, reconciliation.

As my Buddhist friend said, "Jesus trumps everything!"

CHAPTER 9

In Reach

Matthew records Jesus' first message this way: "From that time on Jesus began to preach, 'Repent, for the kingdom of heaven has come near.'"[116]

When Jesus sent the twelve disciples out for their first mission, he said, "As you go, proclaim this message: 'The kingdom of heaven has come near.'"[117] It was so close that it was within their reach.

Jesus carried this same Kingdom theme beyond his disciples. On one occasion Jesus was addressing his remarks to the Pharisees: "The coming of the kingdom of God is not something that can be observed, nor will people say, 'Here it is,' or 'There it is,' because the kingdom of God is in your midst."[118] I think what Jesus is saying is that he has brought the Kingdom—the presence of God—to earth.

So Jesus isn't about the Church and Jesus isn't about Christianity; Jesus is all about the Kingdom among us right here today! After the pre-eminence of Jesus, the presence of the Kingdom is the second essential in breaking down the walls that keep people from Jesus.

Right Here, Right Now

As I've mentioned before, Jesus mentioned the term "church" on only two occasions. He spent most of his time teaching about the Kingdom. But despite his emphasis, we spend most of our time talking about the Church and almost no time talking about the Kingdom.

It's not that we have rejected the Kingdom, but we have reduced it by what we typically teach. There are at least five ways we tend to reduce the Kingdom.

First, we reduce the Kingdom when we call it "mystical." If it's mystical, then it is very difficult to explain and understand definitively. It's sort of otherworldly.

Second, many describe the Kingdom as "heavenly." This is a lot like the first. If the Kingdom is heavenly then it has little, if any, application on earth.

Third, we reduce the Kingdom when we see it as apocalyptic. This means it isn't for today but is relegated to a time in the future when Jesus will set up his Kingdom on earth.

Fourth, we reduce the Kingdom when we equate it to the Church. Many see the Kingdom as the local Church, and therefore the Kingdom is limited by whether the particular Church we have in mind is a good and healthy Church or not.

Finally, we reduce the Kingdom when we define it as acts of social concern. To many, feeding the poor and doing charitable deeds among the needy is where the Kingdom is.

A little bit of each of these dimensions is true, but the Kingdom cannot be defined by any one of them alone. The way Jesus teaches, the Kingdom is greater than anything that has ever existed on earth. Jesus makes it clear that the Kingdom is near—within reach—here and among us right now, and there seems to be a time in the future when the Kingdom will be more fully experienced on earth.

Since Jesus is the King, his teachings and very presence brought the Kingdom to earth for us. Once you embrace the fact that the presence of the Kingdom is right here, right now, you can begin enjoying yourself as you live in the Kingdom right here, right now. You embrace the Kingdom lifestyle by living out the teachings and principles of the King and his Kingdom. Jesus calls it *following him* or *doing the will of the Father* or *hearing his words and* practicing *them*.

In other words, you can live in the Kingdom today, right now. When you embrace the Kingdom lifestyle, you may find yourself going against the grain of the world. (Don't forget that the worldly system Jesus spoke so often about included the religious leadership of the day.) You will find yourself caught up in the flow of the movement of the Kingdom of God or, better yet, you will be caught up in the twenty-first-century Jesus movement. It's a revolutionary movement, and Jesus is the one who leads it.

So see where Jesus is at work and get there as soon as possible. Walk with him. Watch him. Work with him. No matter your circumstances, you can practice the presence of the Kingdom and enjoy the presence of the King—Jesus—right here on planet Earth, right now.

What Is the Kingdom?

A kingdom is where someone rules. Therefore, your kingdom is where you are the king (or queen) of your dome (your world) or domain. Another way of seeing a kingdom is "what you have say over"—all your stuff. Each of us has a kingdom, and you are king or queen over your kingdom. However, when you encounter Jesus, the King of kings, you will want to step down as king and make Jesus your King. So the Kingdom of God is all that God has say over.

I like this simple definition of the Kingdom: wherever the king is, there is the Kingdom. You see, the presence of the Kingdom is the presence of Jesus. If you are going to walk with Jesus—the preeminent one— then it is essential that you walk in his presence, or walk in the presence of the Kingdom where Jesus rules. Walking in the presence of the Kingdom is embracing the principles and teachings of Jesus as a lifestyle.

The Kingdom is not something you build; you must practice it, live it, and be it. It's an alternative reality in this world. In fact, the Kingdom is built into nature—the very structure of our being. It's in our DNA. The Kingdom principles are the principles of life itself. Following these principles is how life works best. In other words, the Kingdom principles of Jesus are not foreign or some new lifestyle in this world. These principles are the way God created everyone to operate from the beginning.

It's like the principle of gravity. On this planet, gravity is in force, no matter how you feel about it or how much you understand about it. According to the principle of gravity, if you jump off a two-story building, you will go down fast and hit with a thud, and you won't like it. No matter what you do, gravity remains in place. You may not understand it, but you must learn to go along with it, or you might get hurt. You can try to break the law of gravity, but it will break you in the process. This is precisely how the principles of the Kingdom of God work.

Once you understand that, you will understand the highly explosive concept of sin in a whole new way. Sin is defined as missing the mark, an arrow falling short of its target. It is not what God created us to do; he wants us to be *on* target. If sin were part of our nature, then we would feel inwardly fulfilled when we sin, without any guilt or regret. But we don't. Sin is an attempt to live against the laws of your being—the principles of the Kingdom—and get away with it.

Sin is missing the mark or falling short. What is the mark we're missing, the standard we're falling short of? It's Jesus. He is the standard. He is the mark. The fullest embodiment of the Kingdom principles is in King Jesus himself. He continues to make known his solution to missing the mark and falling short. His solution is not to believe something new but to change your direction in order to enjoy life to its fullest.

This is really the good news! This is what Jesus calls the gospel, or good news of the Kingdom. This is why the subject of Jesus' first message was "Repent, for the kingdom of heaven has come near."[119] Note what Jesus began to proclaim to the people: "Change your mind about what you're doing—wake up—for the Kingdom of heaven has come near." He begins his teaching with the Kingdom, and ends his teaching with the disciples there.

Jesus went all over, teaching in the local synagogues, proclaiming the good news of the Kingdom. His primary activity to demonstrate Kingdom news was to meet the needs of the people—healing every disease and sickness among them. The message of Jesus was the good news of the Kingdom. Those who were attracted to his message were attracted to the Kingdom. They weren't looking for a new rabbi to come along and plant new synagogues in their villages. These new disciples of Jesus were following Jesus as the King and were thrilled with the message of the Kingdom.

The people of Jesus' time were hoping for the Kingdom but imagined it coming with more of a political impact to get them out from under the Romans. They were missing out on the true good news of the Kingdom, until Jesus came to demonstrate it.

Today, I believe, we are also missing the point of the Kingdom and therefore missing the joy of practicing the presence of the Kingdom here and now. So still, the Kingdom concept is not rejected but rather is reduced from what God intends.

What Do You Have to Do to Enter the Kingdom?

One of the most fascinating things about Jesus' teachings is his perspective on who gets into the Kingdom and who doesn't. There are several aspects to this, and they can be summed up with phrases he used.

Internal righteousness—a matter of the heart. On one occasion Jesus said, "I tell you that unless your righteousness surpasses that of the Pharisees and the teachers of the law, you will certainly not enter the kingdom of heaven."[120]

At the time Jesus walked on earth, the Pharisees and the teachers of the law made an external show of religiosity, but in their hearts was the opposite of what they portrayed. They thought their external show was their ticket to enter the Kingdom of God. Yet Jesus warned about allowing yourself to be caught up in the religiosity of following a list or a system of dos and don'ts, thinking you are impressing God while you are impressing others.

Jesus made it clear that he is not impressed with this kind of thing—so don't you be! Jesus made entering the Kingdom all about the heart.

God is always paying attention to your heart—your inner motivations, your sense of dependence and trust. King David did some very wrong things, yet God saw in David a heart like his own—a heart like God's.[121]

Do the will of my Father. Another time, Jesus said, "Not everyone who says to me, 'Lord, Lord,' will enter the kingdom of heaven, but only the one who does the will of my Father who is in heaven."[122]

If you keep reading, the context is fascinating. Jesus stated, "Many will say to me on that day, 'Lord, Lord, did we not prophesy in your name and in your name drive out demons and in your name perform many miracles?' Then I will tell them plainly, 'I never knew you. Away from me, you evildoers!'"[123]

In the next paragraph Jesus seems to illustrate what he means by "doing the will of my Father" when he says:

> Therefore everyone who hears these words of mine and puts them into practice is like a wise man who built his house on the rock. The rain came down, the streams rose, and the winds blew and beat against that house; yet it did not fall, because it had its foundation on the rock. But everyone who hears these words of mine and does not put them into practice is like a foolish man who built his house on sand. The rain came down, the streams rose, and the winds blew and beat against that house, and it fell with a great crash.[124]

It seems that only those who hear the words of Jesus and put them into practice will enter the Kingdom.

Be like a child. Jesus again said, "I tell you the truth, unless you change and become like little children, you will never enter the kingdom of heaven."[125] In a different context, during his interaction with Nicodemus, Jesus used another metaphor to say the same thing. "Very truly I tell you, no one can see the kingdom of God unless they are born again. . . . No one can enter the kingdom of God unless they are born of water and the Spirit." He went on to say: "Flesh gives birth to flesh, but the Spirit gives birth to spirit."[126]

Being "born again" is essentially illustrating his theme of being like a child. As a very religious man, Nicodemus had too many add-ons; therefore, he needed to be born all over again in order to be like a little child, so that he could enter the Kingdom.

As a spiritual child, you want to learn all you can about this new life with Jesus. As a spiritual child, you need to learn the ABCs of walking with Jesus. As a spiritual child, it's most helpful to watch Jesus carefully and mimic what you hear and see. As a spiritual child, you want to learn to simply trust Jesus with your life.

Difficult for a rich person to enter. Jesus made this statement after talking with a rich young man. Let's back up and see the story unfold.

A man came up to Jesus and asked, "Teacher, what good thing must I do to get eternal life?"

"Why do you ask me about what is good?" Jesus replied. "There is only One who is good. If you want to enter life, keep the commandments."

"Which ones?" he inquired.

Jesus replied, "'You shall not murder, you shall not commit adultery, you shall not steal, you shall not give false testimony, honor your father and mother,' and 'love your neighbor as yourself.'"[127]

In other words, Jesus equated eternal life with entering life or really living, then later spoke of entering the Kingdom of God.

The young man asserted:

> "All these I have kept. . . . What do I still lack?"
>
> Jesus answered, "If you want to be perfect, go, sell your possessions and give to the poor, and you will have treasure in heaven. Then come, follow me."[128]

By "perfect," Jesus meant to be complete and whole in your search for life.

Then Jesus made the following observation: "I tell you the truth, it is hard for a rich man to enter the kingdom of heaven."[129] To drive home his point even more strongly, he said, "Again I tell you, it is easier for a camel [or rope, in some translations] to go through the eye of a needle than for a rich man to enter the kingdom of God."[130]

Whether the image here truly is a camel or a rope going through the eye of a needle, the essence of what Jesus is saying is still the same. It is impossible for a rich person to enter into the Kingdom through his or her performance and wealth. The difficulty for rich people is that they tend to trust in their riches for security and tend to think that people, places, and things can make them happy or whole and complete.

Jesus' words astonished the disciples. They asked, "Who then can be saved?"[131]

Jesus looked at them and said, "With man this [being saved or entering the Kingdom] is impossible, but with God all things are possible."[132]

Do you want to enter the Kingdom of God? What or who do you depend on—your bank account, your stuff, or God? If you are rich and have a lot of stuff, then hold on to that stuff loosely, so that you are not trusting in your riches but in God for a complete and full eternal life and entrance into the Kingdom.

Sinners will enter first. The final reference Jesus made concerning what it takes to enter or not enter the Kingdom of God has a couple of dimensions, both direct warnings toward the religious.

Here's the first dimension. Jesus said to the religious leaders, "I tell you the truth, the tax collectors and the prostitutes are entering the kingdom of God ahead of you. For John came to you to show you the way of righteousness, and you did not believe him, but the tax collectors and the prostitutes did. And even after you saw this, you did not repent and believe him."[133]

Jesus became most disturbed and angry with those who didn't see their need for God—those who thought they were right and righteous because of their beliefs and practices. Those who see their need most are the ones who are actually entering the Kingdom right now ahead of the religious and the righteous. He is not just saying that the most despised tax collectors and prostitutes will enter the Kingdom someday, but that they are entering right now!

Now for the second dimension: Jesus said on another occasion, "Woe to you, teachers of the law and Pharisees, you hypocrites! You shut the kingdom of heaven in men's faces. You yourselves do not enter, nor will you let those enter who are trying to."[134]

Note the specifics of what Jesus is saying here in Matthew 23. He is clearly saying that the religious people in positions of authority were not entering the Kingdom. He had made several observations at other times about the reasons why they would not enter the Kingdom. Primarily it was their religious pride—they thought they knew it all and were always right.

Jesus pointed out that these religious leaders who were not entering the Kingdom were also stopping others from entering by shutting the door of the Kingdom of heaven in their faces. How did they do this? I think they did it by continually setting up certain restrictions (hurdles or add-ons) and limitations on who could get in and who would not.

I did the same thing as a teenager. I had been taught that no one could come into a relationship with God unless you go down front at the end of a Church service. In many discussions with my friends, I made this clear to them. The man-made rule I had embraced served to be a major barrier to my friends being attracted to Jesus.

To sum up, Jesus was saying those who don't have it together will enter the Kingdom first. Those who think they have it all together through what they know and believe and what they do may not enter the Kingdom at all. And these religious "know-it-alls" tend to turn people off, which essentially shuts others out of the Kingdom too.

A couple of thoughts here:

- Don't deceive yourself into thinking that your religious system or your behavior will get you into the Kingdom.
- Don't divert others away from Jesus because of your dogmatic religious system.

Stick with the teachings and principles of Jesus. If Jesus says this or that is important in order to enter the Kingdom, then go with him on it.

So, What Does Jesus Want Us to Do with the Organized Church?

Jesus didn't come to launch the organized Church as we know it. He came to launch a movement—the Jesus movement, which is the Kingdom of God.

The Jesus movement is the natural result of people who are following Jesus. They are moving with Jesus and with one another. The Kingdom is the rule of God on planet Earth, both personally and in community. The church is a simple gathering together.

The term "church" is not a special or holy word, as many believe and teach. It literally means "called-out ones" and was used to describe city council meetings or any kind of assembly where people are called out to meet for a purpose. In a religious context, it simply is a gathering of followers of Jesus.

The simple gathering of followers of Jesus on any day and at any location is a church. These gatherings revolve around four ingredients— fellowship, food, prayer, and the apostles' teachings.[135]

So, since the Kingdom is the rule and presence of God on planet Earth, think of it this way: wherever the King is, there is the Kingdom. The King and the Kingdom are inseparable. Therefore, a good way to view the Kingdom is Jesus-likeness universalized. Being like Jesus—walking, talking, loving, and thinking like Jesus—is Kingdom living.

To help you get the picture of what the Kingdom is like, check out the following comparisons between the Kingdom and the Church.

The Kingdom is universal. The Church is local. A Church consists of a gathering of followers of Jesus who are seeking, sharing in, and spreading the message of Jesus and his Kingdom. The Church is not everywhere but rather is localized and limited to those who choose to gather together. The Kingdom is everywhere and unlimited in its impact on society. The Kingdom is not waiting for a local gathering to be established in order to have its effect. The Kingdom is already there in every country and in every culture.

The Church tends to be an organization. The Kingdom tends to be a movement.

Jesus speaks of the good news of the Kingdom, but he never speaks of the good news of the organized Church.

The Kingdom is invisible. The organized Church is visible.

You must *go* to the Church. The Kingdom *goes with you* wherever you go.

The Church gathers and scatters. The Kingdom is always present with you.

You enter the Church by membership. You enter the Kingdom by following Jesus.

Jesus never commanded anyone to seek the Church. Jesus commanded everyone who follows him to seek the Kingdom.

The Church may or may not grow. The Kingdom is continually growing. Therefore, the Church can be shut down, but the Kingdom cannot be.

The Church may have God present. The Kingdom is God's presence in those who follow Jesus.

Reading through the five Gospels (Matthew, Mark, Luke, John, and Acts), it is clear what Jesus and the disciples did with the "organized Church." View the synagogue as the organized Church. There are three observations that seem most relevant to me.

- You don't find Jesus or the disciples bashing the synagogue (Church).
- You don't find Jesus or the disciples starting new synagogues (Churches) because of inadequate teaching or worship.
- You find Jesus and the disciples going to the synagogues (Churches) and then orbiting around them.

Several years ago, I read a book called *Orbiting the Giant Hairball: A Corporate Fool's Guide to Surviving with Grace* by Gordon MacKenzie.[136] MacKenzie worked at Hallmark for thirty years in the creative department, writing greeting cards. He found that he was unable to be very creative if he had to spend his time in corporate meetings. So he learned to orbit around the corporate bureaucracy and not be entangled in it, freeing himself to create. But in the book he also makes it clear that the hairball was necessary. Without it, there was nothing to power the orbit. And the hairball paid the bills.

This is exactly what the early fellowships of Jesus did. They participated in the synagogue, yet they were in orbit around their synagogue, around their communities, and around the marketplace. They went to synagogue (Church) every Sabbath, yet they were there for a higher purpose—a Kingdom purpose. They were there to introduce more and more people to the preeminence of Jesus. When others expressed interest, they invited them to eat together and practiced the presence of the Kingdom.

Most Churches today realize how important it is to move their members into a smaller gathering, so they put a lot of energy into small groups. Some of these small groups practice the preeminence of Jesus and the presence of the Kingdom and some don't. If the groups gather in the name of Jesus and become more like family, Jesus shows up and great things happen. Small groups that are only study groups or small lecture groups tend to learn about Jesus and not get to know Jesus and his Kingdom community.

The Jesus movement is global. God is calling people from every culture of the world to personal transformation. I believe God is doing this through the irresistible Jesus and the irreversible Kingdom.

The Presence of the Kingdom

The preeminence of Jesus, the King, and the presence of the Kingdom are inseparable.

Jesus' character is the core of the Kingdom presence. The Kingdom is the only moral authority with any kind of power to change society. The organized Church is not capable of it. The Church changes from time to time. Sometimes it's effective and sometimes it's not. Leaders are morally good and leaders are morally flawed. So, at any given time, the Church will not be able to deliver an ongoing moral authority to the community. The Kingdom is constant. Its power and effectiveness depend upon its leader—Jesus. Therefore, living in the Kingdom and inviting others to share in it is the only solution to transforming a broken culture.

Jesus' teachings lead to fulfillment and meaning in the Kingdom. Jesus is the ultimate standard, and the Kingdom is the lifestyle of living this out in society. The lifestyle of Kingdom living is where ultimate fulfillment and meaning reside. They are the laws of the universe. Living outside the laws of the Kingdom is not what the Creator intended for your fulfillment. For instance, one of the laws of the Kingdom is to forgive those who have hurt you. If you refuse to live out this Kingdom principle, you will pay dearly for it. You will be bound by your lack of forgiveness. You will be eaten up with this unforgiving heart. By breaking the principle, you are broken. When living within the Kingdom, you are safe and free and most fulfilled.

The presence of God is within the Kingdom. Where better to discover a personal relationship with the God of gods than where He lives in His Kingdom. Most people only go to Church at baptisms, marriages, and funerals—only to be hatched, matched, and dispatched. Followers of Jesus practice the presence of the Kingdom every day. The church of Jesus, where his followers gather, has the opportunity to touch the people in our world where they are living, rather than always inviting them to come to organized Church, where they may or may not be spiritually touched at all. With this kind of practice of the Kingdom lifestyle there are massive opportunities to plant the seeds of Jesus everywhere—his peace, his joy, his love, and his grace.

This is the original intent of the movement Jesus came to launch. It's simple! It's Jesus and his Kingdom!

Follow the King . . . and you'll discover the Kingdom.

Embrace the Kingdom lifestyle . . . and you'll find yourself in the arms of the King!

CHAPTER 10

Secrets of the Kingdom

One day, in the spirit of fully embodying the Kingdom on earth and bringing freedom to all he encountered, Jesus healed a man who was demonized in such a way that the man could neither see nor speak. Since this was one of the miracles the people thought the Messiah would perform, it was too threatening for those in power within the Jewish leadership. When Jesus performed this incredible miracle, the Pharisees and the leadership attributed his work to the devil—Beelzebub.[137]

With the rejection of Jesus by the religious authorities, the disciples had to be very discouraged and their hopes dashed. They had been riding high, following and promoting their candidate for the new leader of the Jews, who would surely put an end to the Roman domination. His popularity was skyrocketing. Until now.

With this in mind, the disciples (the many followers of Jesus, not just the twelve) must have asked this question of Jesus: "What's the Kingdom going to look like now?" In order to communicate the principles of the Kingdom, Jesus shifted into a new form of teaching, called *parables*, or visual stories.

Everyone noticed the difference in Jesus' approach, and the disciples asked about it: "Why do you speak to the people in parables?"[138]

Allow me to quote his response at some length. He said:

> The knowledge of the secrets of the kingdom of heaven has been given to you, but not to them. Those who have will be given more, and they will have an abundance. As for those who do not have, even what they have will be taken from them. This is why I speak to them in parables:
>
> > "Though seeing, they do not see;
> > > though hearing, they do not hear or understand."
>
> In them is fulfilled the prophecy of Isaiah:
> > "You will be ever hearing but never understanding;
> > > you will be ever seeing but never perceiving.
> > For this people's heart has become calloused;
> > > they hardly hear with their ears,
> > > and they have closed their eyes.
> > Otherwise they might see with their eyes,
> > > hear with their ears,
> > > understand with their hearts and turn,
> > and I would heal them."
>
> But blessed are your eyes because they see, and your ears because they hear. Truly I tell you, many prophets and righ-

teous people longed to see what you see but did not see it, and to hear what you hear but did not hear it.[139]

Jesus revealed two purposes for shifting into teaching in parables. The first was that he wanted his disciples to know about the Kingdom, because they had ears to hear and eyes to see—in other words, they were leaning in and interested. The other purpose was to conceal these principles from those who weren't interested or leaning in—those who didn't have eyes to see or ears to hear. In a way, this was a compassionate thing for Jesus to do. To continue to heap truth on those who were already rejecting it was to pile up more and more condemnation on these people. This takes us back to the basic principle that God only requires that we be interested and lean in; then we will see and hear more.

Matthew records eight parables at the beginning of this shift in Jesus' manner of teaching. We'll look at each one. Together, they teach us how to understand and live in the Kingdom today.

The Parable of the Soils

Jesus set the tone of his parabolic teaching with the parable of the soils:

> A farmer went out to sow his seed. As he was scattering the seed, some fell along the path, and the birds came and ate it up. Some fell on rocky places, where it did not have much soil. It sprang up quickly, because the soil was shallow. But when the sun came up, the plants were scorched, and they withered because they had no root. Other seed fell among

thorns, which grew up and choked the plants. Still other seed fell on good soil, where it produced a crop—a hundred, sixty or thirty times what was sown. Whoever has ears, let them hear.[140]

Next, Jesus explained this parable:

Listen then to what the parable of the sower means: When people hear the message about the kingdom and do not understand it, the evil one comes and snatches away what was sown in their hearts. This is the seed sown along the path. The seed falling on rocky ground refers to people who hear the word and at once receive it with joy. But since they have no root, they last only a short time. When trouble or persecution comes because of the word, they quickly fall away. The seed falling among the thorns refers to people who hear the word, but the worries of this life and the deceitfulness of wealth choke the word, making it unfruitful. But the seed falling on good soil refers to people who hear the word and understand it. They produce a crop, yielding a hundred, sixty or thirty times what was sown.[141]

In Matthew's version of this teaching, Jesus says that he is the sower. When Jesus was physically on the earth, his words were pitched out to those who listened to him. Today, Jesus is still sowing the seed, but now he is doing it through our lives and through the stories of those who are following him.

Sowing seed during Jesus' time was not like taking a package of seeds and carefully putting them in the ground; it was a scattering method, usually throwing the seed out by hand. Therefore, the sowing was indiscriminate and the seed was in essence planted everywhere. This is why some seed landed in different places—beside the road, on rocky places, among the thorns, and on the good soil.

Jesus referred to the seed sown in three ways: The seed is the "word." The seed is the "message about the kingdom." The seed is the "people of the kingdom."[142]

Jesus seemed to view the seed sown in and through the people of the Kingdom as the word of God and the message of God's Kingdom. This was his primary message as he taught throughout the villages and synagogues. Therefore, the word of God—the message of the Kingdom—is the active presence of God, working within, among, and through the followers of Jesus in the form of a seed.

This seed has tremendous spiritual power to be productive within those who are followers of Jesus. It is able to produce amazing levels of fruit. To be fruitful is to enjoy the peace, joy, love, and grace of Jesus for yourself. And if you as a follower show up, you can bring that same fruit for those in need.

The effect on you and through you is determined by your response to the seed. It's all a matter of responsiveness. Note that you are not responsible to bring forth the fruit, but to provide good, receptive soil for the seed; the power of the seed will produce the fruit if planted in the good soil. I've come to realize that the soil metaphor is dynamic in our lives. I have been each of these soils at one time or another. Can you see this in your life as well?

This answers what I see with people who seem to "get it," yet fade away. This also answers what I see with people who all of a sudden "get it" after they have been around this sowing for years.

Now, here is what impresses me most about this teaching. Jesus was saying that if you have ears to hear and eyes to see, you are receptive to the good news of the Kingdom. And in this receptive mode Jesus measured the fruitfulness by thirty-, sixty-, and one hundredfold. Fruitfulness is basically the spiritual growth and maturity in your own life and the effects of your life on others around you. He began with thirty—multiplying by thirty times the yield of a normal crop. So this means that the lowest level of fruitfulness will be outstanding. Then he went on to say you may enjoy multiples of that, even to the point of sixty and one hundredfold. That's incredible—beyond belief!

Out of all of the eight parables recorded in Matthew 13, only one parable has an action step to it. There is one primary activity within the Kingdom that Jesus came to establish. It's right here in the parable of the soils. The primary activity of the Kingdom is the constant sowing of the seed of the good news of the Kingdom.

Please note: the primary activity is *not* trying to get people to go to heaven.

It is *not* trying to convert people to join a certain religion.

It is *not* trying to get people to join your religious organization.

The primary activity is the sowing of seed—introducing the word of God, the good news of the Kingdom, which is present and alive within and among the followers of Jesus.

The primary activity is introducing people to the Person of Jesus—without all the religious baggage.

After the parable of the soils, Jesus introduced seven additional parables. Each one is more descriptive of what the Kingdom is like and offers a picture of the nature of the Kingdom of God on earth.

Remember, all of the parables are presented to answer the question in the minds of his disciples, "What's the Kingdom going to look like, now that the Jewish leadership has rejected Jesus as God's Messiah?" Each parable is a description of the Kingdom that Jesus came to establish.

The Parable of the Weeds

The second parable goes like this:

> The kingdom of heaven is like a man who sowed good seed in his field. But while everyone was sleeping, his enemy came and sowed weeds among the wheat, and went away. When the wheat sprouted and formed heads, then the weeds also appeared.
>
> The owner's servants came to him and said, "Sir, didn't you sow good seed in your field? Where then did the weeds come from?"
>
> "An enemy did this," he replied.
>
> The servants asked him, "Do you want us to go and pull them up?"
>
> "No," he answered, "because while you are pulling the weeds, you may uproot the wheat with them. Let both grow together until the harvest. At that time I will tell the harvesters: First collect the weeds and tie them in bundles to be burned; then gather the wheat and bring it into my barn."[143]

Jesus said that there will be genuine wheat and weeds growing side by side in the Kingdom. The Kingdom consists of the weeds (the bad seed) growing alongside the genuine wheat (the good seed). When one is caught up in the work of sowing, there will likely be a discovery of weeds that are sown alongside the wheat. These "weeds" are literally empty wheat pods—chaff without wheat kernels. So it's false wheat that looks like wheat but isn't.

The genuine wheat plants are those who believe in the gospel of the Kingdom, and the weeds are those who look good but are not genuine followers of Jesus. They are all together in the same field, and it may be difficult to tell the difference.

The servants' tendency is to want to remove the weeds out of the wheat field—to separate the wheat from the weeds. But the owner quickly responds, "Let both grow together until the harvest," the reason being that if one attempts to pull out the weeds from the wheat, there's a great likelihood that the genuine wheat will also be pulled out. In other words, it is none of our business who is *in* and who is *out*.

Only Jesus knows for sure!

The Parable of the Mustard Seed

Jesus continued: "The kingdom of heaven is like a mustard seed, which a man took and planted in his field. Though it is the smallest of all seeds, yet when it grows, it is the largest of garden plants and becomes a tree, so that the birds come and perch in its branches."[144]

Jesus was saying here that the Kingdom will experience incredible growth. It may seem very small and insignificant at the beginning, yet it will grow immensely. You can count on that and be encouraged by it.

No Church, mosque, or temple can count on this kind of growth. The Kingdom of God can!

Another way to look at this is that the Kingdom is a completely different thing. The Kingdom is invisible. Because you can't see it, you don't expect a massive growth, but it occurs silently and pervasively. The Kingdom can penetrate any culture and supersedes any organization, no matter how large or active it may be. The Kingdom's incredible growth can only be explained by the power of God. No man-made program can do any better. No man-made program has *ever* done any better.

The Parable of the Yeast

The next parable in line is this: "The kingdom of heaven is like yeast that a woman took and mixed into about sixty pounds of flour until it worked all through the dough."[145]

Once the leaven or yeast is introduced into the dough, it spreads everywhere throughout the lump. What's interesting is that it cannot be stopped. Once it is introduced, it cannot be removed. So the teaching here is that Kingdom growth will be irreversible, once introduced into a person, a community, a society, or a nation. Nothing will be able to stop it. Nothing and no one can stop it from spreading—not communism, fascism, racism, or any other *–isms*. When the Kingdom spreads, it supersedes all sorts of movements and organizations. This is why, to follow Jesus most effectively, it's important to be a Kingdom person first and foremost.

To be anything else is to be so much less!

You know what's interesting? The movement of the Kingdom goes on, no matter what you or I think, say, or do. Our primary responsibility is not to make something happen but to see where Jesus is at work and go there to join him in the work already in progress. Remember, it's irreversible! It cannot be stopped.

The Parables of the Hidden Treasure and the Pearl

Parables five and six are best looked at together, just as they appear in the text: "The kingdom of heaven is like treasure hidden in a field. When a man found it, he hid it again, and then in his joy went and sold all he had and bought that field. Again, the kingdom of heaven is like a merchant looking for fine pearls. When he found one of great value, he went away and sold everything he had and bought it."[146]

These two parables are similar yet different.

The similarity between the two seems to be this: When people hear the message of the Kingdom and receive it, they become convinced that the Kingdom is the most valuable thing they've ever heard. Therefore, they are willing to sell everything to possess it.

The difference between the two seems to be this: The man who finds the hidden treasure in the field, hides it again, and sells all he has to buy that field is a person who comes into the Kingdom *by surprise*. He is so filled with joy because he wasn't even looking for it. The merchant who is looking for fine pearls finds the best one ever and sells everything he has to buy that pearl. He is the person who comes into the Kingdom *by searching*, knowing its value.

So people will come into the Kingdom in all sorts of ways, but ultimately either by searching or surprise.

Note that both men in the parables have the same response. They each sell all they have and buy their newfound treasure. This has nothing to do with purchasing or performing well enough to gain a place in the Kingdom. But it has everything to do with the incomparable value of being with the King in the Kingdom rather than just going through the motions, living a life that is routine and predictable with all of the traditional comforts of life—all without the King and outside the Kingdom.

So, how do you value your relationship with the King and his Kingdom? Is it the most valuable place to be, ever? Or is it just a pleasant place to visit from time to time?

This is the difference between being a spectator and a participant!

The Parable of the Net

With the next parable, the analogy shifts yet again, to a profession some of Jesus' followers knew well.

> Once again, the kingdom of heaven is like a net that was let down into the lake and caught all kinds of fish. When it was full, the fishermen pulled it up on the shore. Then they sat down and collected the good fish in baskets, but threw the bad away. This is how it will be at the end of the age. The angels will come and separate the wicked from the righteous and throw them into the blazing furnace, where there will be weeping and gnashing of teeth.[147]

Jesus wanted to make certain his disciples understood that there will be a sorting and that he will be in charge of it. His disciples didn't have to do any sorting whatsoever. In fact, it's clear that no follower of Jesus can do anything with respect to the ultimate results of who are the wicked and who are the righteous.

Note the term "wicked" that Jesus frequently uses. He isn't speaking of a vile, despicable person, but "wicked" is used of those who do not hear or welcome the words of Jesus and do not practice them.

The primary issue here for me is that the parable of the net teaches us that there will be an accounting at the end. And that everyone will be caught in the net for the final accounting.

The Parable of the Scribe

Finally comes the last of the eight parables in Matthew 13, a parable that has been so easily overlooked. I've overlooked it until recently. Take a fresh look for yourself:

> Every teacher of the law who has been instructed about the kingdom of heaven is like the owner of a house who brings out of his storeroom new treasures as well as old.[148]

Jesus is referring to a person who is a teacher of the Law—one who knows the Law well. Then this one who is conversant with the Law is taught the message of the Kingdom of heaven. A person in this position is like the owner of a house who is able to share with his guests new things (things of the Kingdom) as well as the old things (the Law).

In fact, what our little core group is discovering is that walking with Jesus in the Kingdom lifestyle brings something new and fresh every day. Personally, my learning curve isn't a curve anymore; it's perpendicular! It's the most thrilling adventure ever!

The Power of the Seed

As Jesus made the shift into teaching by way of parables, he laid a foundation for understanding the Kingdom principles for those who have ears to hear and eyes to see. Several helpful factors stand out: The most powerful element of the Kingdom lifestyle exists in a seed, and a very small one at that. Therefore, the power of the Kingdom is not what is readily seen. It's invisible, imperceptible, and yet indelible in its markings on those who follow after Jesus and those they touch.

The second most important element of this Kingdom lifestyle is that it requires each follower to prepare his or her heart to receive the seed in order to establish its root, develop a shoot, and bear fruit. Even as I say that, I realize that preparation of the heart may be more what you don't do than what you do.

- That you *don't* allow the trials and troubles that come against you to distract you from having a receptive heart—that is, leaning into the ways of Jesus and the Kingdom

- That you *don't* get caught up in worrying about your life and your world

- That you *don't* allow the riches of this world to deceive you into thinking they are more important than walking in the ways of Jesus and the Kingdom lifestyle

If you *don't* do these things, you will be able to keep your soil receptive to the seed of the word of God—the message of the Kingdom.

Jesus revealed the secrets of the Kingdom—the secrets to living life most fully with him and his principles. Jesus revealed the mystery of the Kingdom lifestyle. Remember, the principles of the Kingdom are actually the principles of life. Jesus' teachings are primarily about the Kingdom way of life. If you get into the flow of the Kingdom way of life, you will experience the greatest personal and relational satisfaction possible, no matter what comes your way.

This is not only the *right* way to live your life; it's the *best* way!

More importantly, it is Jesus' way.

He plants a seed in the soil of your heart. Then he waits, knowing that in time the seed will germinate, take root, and eventually transform you. From the inside out!

CHAPTER 11

The Power of the Few

The three essentials to understanding Jesus as simply enough are:

- The preeminence of Jesus—making the main thing the main thing
- The presence of the Kingdom—embracing the principles of Jesus as a lifestyle
- The power of the few

The first two essentials are most effectively activated in the third—the power of the few. This may be the most counterintuitive dimension within the Jesus movement. The power of the few contains the same core idea as the seed. Just as the seed is small and seemingly insignificant, proving to become large, irreversible in its growth, and powerful enough to accomplish inner transformation, so it is with the power of the few.

The primary example of the power of the few is found in Jesus' method of operation. Instead of using Madison Avenue marketing methods, Jesus launched his movement with a few people. Just three, to be exact—Peter, James, and John. Then he selected nine more. After that, he sent out seventy-two in pairs to carry the message of the Kingdom.

Although Jesus spoke to large groups from time to time, he mostly hung out with a few at a time. Jesus knew that by working with a few who really "got it," the power of that few would be revolutionary!

I will soon get to Jesus' own words about his strategy of building into the few—in his case, the twelve disciples. But first, let's look at an example from early Church history. It shows us why the power of the few is a power we should be looking to access today.

The Blueprint for Worldwide Revolution

I have asked a question over and over of pastors, professors, counselors, Bible students, and hundreds of other people at gatherings. The question is simple. After having them silently read the first chapter of 1 Thessalonians, I ask, "Who wrote First Thessalonians?"

No one has given me the correct answer yet. Everyone answers, "Paul!"

I did the same thing when I was first asked this question. However, in the very first verse this book clearly says who wrote it. It was Paul, Silvanus (Silas), and Timothy. These three wrote the book. And it was the dynamic relationship of these three men, not just Paul, that the Thessalonians imitated. These three men practiced the principle of the power of the few, and their work proved to be most effective and most powerful.

Their ministry followed Jesus' pattern of walking together as a few and echoed forth from the believers in Thessalonica throughout Greece and much of the rest of the world. The Thessalonians were known for their faith that worked (work of faith), their love that worked (labor of love), and their hope that persevered (steadfastness of hope).[149] The citizens of Thessalonica saw something so unusual that it persuaded them to turn away from idols to serve the living and true God and to wait for Jesus to return.[150]

The most shocking thing about their response is how it all began. The history of Paul, Silas, and Timothy's work among the Thessalonians is recorded in Acts 17:1–9. These three men, walking with Jesus and with one another, were putting into practice the promise that Jesus had given them: "Where two or three come together in my name, there am I with them."[151]

When these three men walked together in Jesus, he showed up powerfully. They were practicing the power of the few. They really got it, and it was so evident that it spread contagiously.

An explosion occurred in the hearts of many in Thessalonica that was inspired by the transforming power of Jesus seen in these three men. This is what is often termed the "spontaneous expansion" of the community of Jesus. And this explosion spread like wildfire. Note that the spontaneous expansion of the Jesus community was spread by word of mouth—no TV or radio broadcasts, no podcasts, no Internet, no sermons on CDs. And by the way, it is the same today. The best way to spread the message of Jesus and the Kingdom is by word of mouth—a life-on-life experience through a few who "get it."

When Paul, Silas, and Timothy entered the city of Thessalonica, they met all sorts of people, who worshiped a variety of gods and their corresponding idols. They stuck to their message of Jesus and the Kingdom and experienced an amazing response that spread throughout Asia Minor. The good news of Jesus and the Kingdom is spread through a few who have been transformed by the power of Jesus.

Not only did Jesus and his followers use the power of the few most effectively, but today those who follow Jesus follow that same pattern. The power of the few is what many have always sought within the organized

Church when they feel the need to promote small groups of any kind. But even a small group may not get the results we're talking about in the "power of the few." The real dynamic of the power of the few is genuine fellowship—participation in one another's lives in such a way as to develop a personal support system. This support system becomes so strengthening that it serves as an inner security system. I am stronger as I live my life in relationship with other brothers and sisters who are followers of Jesus.

In the past, I've spent so much energy producing the best possible speeches to the masses. However, I always knew that, upon hearing me speak, only 5 percent really get it, 15 percent think they get it, and 80 percent remain somewhere in the fog with no idea what was said. Oh, they will remember an illustration or two or a joke or two, but they will likely miss the essential point of the message. Now that I am into the power of the few, I am discovering that the few really do get it and embrace it for themselves. You see, when someone really gets what it means to walk with Jesus in his Kingdom presence, the message becomes contagious. To me, the power of the few is a must for all who are serious about following Jesus, *simply* Jesus.

The Power of the Few in My Own Life

As I have given up living my life on my own, making up my own mind, making my own decisions, organizing and planning the next steps for my life, I have come to a new strength and confidence walking with a few others. Walking with others who are committed to following Jesus empowers me with four vital things in my life:

I am empowered with the love and acceptance that I experience in this group. They know me best and love me the most.

I am empowered to be a more balanced person. I want to follow Jesus, yet this is the toughest thing I've ever attempted to do. Left to my own devices and thinking, I push my old default buttons of taking control and leaving Jesus out of the conversation. My dear friends in this group sharpen my thinking and my resolve to keep on track with Jesus. This happens weekly. I learn so much by walking with a few.

I am empowered to be stronger as I go out from this group. There is something about walking with a few who are going the same direction that becomes strength as you go. I know I am being sent out each week to represent Jesus and the Kingdom from this group that is praying for me and wants to know how it's going throughout the week.

I am empowered knowing that, no matter what happens in my life, I have a group of brothers and sisters who are there for me. We actually see it as doing life together. If there is a crisis in the middle of the night, that group will be there.

By the way, this group is not only empowering to *me*; we are there for *one another.* We've gone through several struggles with cancer, addictions, trouble with our kids, working with the homeless, dealing with the death of two of our little core group. We walk daily in agreement in the name of Jesus—never alone—and it works!

But my understanding of the power of the few emanates from more than anecdotal observations. According to Jesus, it is irrefutably tied to the work his Father sent him to do.

The Finished Work of Jesus

At the close of Jesus' work with his disciples, Jesus prayed earnestly to his Father. Jesus prayed concerning himself. Jesus prayed concerning his early disciples. Jesus prayed concerning all those who would become his followers in the future.[152] It's within this prayer that Jesus unveiled the original plan behind the power of the few. What makes the power of the few so revolutionary is that working with the few is the unlikely key to reaching the masses, because working with a few who really get it is life changing for the few and the many.

On the cross, one of Jesus' last statements was "It is finished."[153] I believe that in addition to referring to finishing the work of redemption on the cross, this refers to his work with his disciples. Check out what Jesus said about his finished work in his prayer on the night before he died. It's within these words of Jesus' prayer in John 17 that we find the true, revolutionary nature of what Jesus came to do and what he expects from his followers.

> This is eternal life, that they may know You, the only true God, and Jesus Christ whom You have sent. I glorified You on the earth, having accomplished the work which You have given Me to do. . . . I have manifested Your name to the men whom You gave Me out of the world; they were Yours and You gave them to Me, and they have kept Your word.
>
> Now they have come to know that everything You have given Me is from You; for the words which You gave Me I have given to them; and they received them and truly understood that I came forth from You, and they believed that You sent Me. . . .
>
> I am no longer in the world; and *yet* they themselves are in the world, and I come to You. Holy Father, keep them in

Your name, the name which You have given me, that they may be one even as We are. While I was with them, I was keeping them in Your name which You have given Me. . . . But now I come to You; and these things I speak in the world so that they may have My joy made full in themselves. I have given them Your word. . . . Sanctify [set apart] them in the truth; Your word is truth. As You sent Me into the world, I also have sent them into the world. . . .

I do not ask on behalf of these alone, but for those also who believe in Me through their word; that they may all be one; even as You, Father, are in Me and I in You, that they also may be in Us, so that the world may believe that You sent Me.

The glory which You have given Me I have given to them, that they may be one, just as We are one; I in them and You in me, that they may be perfected in unity, so that the world may know that You sent me, and loved them, even as You have loved Me. . . .

O righteous Father, although the world has not known You, yet I have known You; and these have known that You sent Me; and I have made Your name known to them, and will make it known, so that the love with which You loved Me may be in them, and I in them.[154]

Several things stand out to me from the words of Jesus recorded in John 17:

The revolutionary work Jesus came to accomplish was to share with his disciples certain words from the Father. Wow! If we only knew what these "words" were that the Father gave Jesus to share with the disciples, we could continue this as the work Jesus is still accomplishing today![155]

Well, I think we *do* know what those words are, certainly for the most part. These words are recorded for us in the five Gospels—Matthew, Mark, Luke, John, and Acts. So maybe it makes sense to focus most of our energies in learning what Jesus shared with his disciples in order to embrace the revolutionary work of Jesus.

The revolutionary work Jesus came to accomplish was to be done with a few. Jesus, in his infinite wisdom, saw that it would be most effective to work with a few as he shared what the Father sent him to share. He was not tempted to share it with the masses, because he knew that they wouldn't "get it." In fact, it took a long time for the few to "get it."

By going to the masses, Jesus would have produced hearers of the word who deceived themselves, rather than doers of the word.[156] Think about it. Most truly transformational experiences in your life and mine have come in relationship with a few. So, if that is true (and I'm convinced it is), why aren't we more compelled to share with others in such a way that they can have the same transformational experience? The power of the few, or the context of community, is necessary for people to experience authentic transformation as they follow Jesus.

The revolutionary work Jesus came to accomplish was to be different from the world system already in place. Jesus, as the King of kings, came to establish his Kingdom on earth with those who become his disciples on the earth. This Kingdom is not separate from the earth, but it is different from it. Check it out. What Jesus shared seems to most always be just the opposite of what the world system is today and just the opposite of what we feel is the natural thing to do. Instead of buying and selling being the primary theme, Jesus teaches giving and receiving. Instead of getting even, Jesus teaches the supernatural power of forgiveness. Instead of avoiding pain and suffering, Jesus teaches to embrace your pain and suffering so that you will emerge more whole. Instead of being repulsed by the poor, diseased, and disabled, Jesus teaches to go to them and extend his love to them. Instead of going with the crowd, Jesus teaches us to stand with him and his people. Instead of loving the masses in general (whatever that means), Jesus teaches us to love *one another*—on a personal level.

Note something even more significant about the teachings of Jesus. Jesus didn't just teach these dynamic principles and thoughts; he lived them out. He forgave, he healed, he touched, and he hurt with those in need.

The revolutionary work Jesus came to accomplish was to be passed on by his disciples to others over the generations to come. Jesus came to share these "words" from the Father to those who will share these "words" with others. He even prayed for those who would believe through these first few for generations to come. It's just that simple. The message of Jesus is fully expressed when one learns to pass it on. To put it another way: the one who teaches another learns twice!

The revolutionary work Jesus came to accomplish will result in his disciples having his joy made full in them and being loved the same way the Father loved Jesus—all wrapped up in one another in a unique oneness of the Father, Jesus, and the disciples. This makes it all worth being a revolutionary with Jesus. You will know what it means to have his full joy and you will be enveloped in his love and the love of the Father. These two results will encourage you to continue, allowing Jesus' finished work to work itself out through you.

I have known this joy and this love from time to time in my life, but not on a continual basis—until Jesus took hold of my life in a new and very real way. This is what makes this life of practicing Kingdom principles and acting as revolutionaries in the name of Jesus such an enjoyable adventure.

The revolutionary work Jesus came to accomplish is not limited to the first twelve disciples but is also for those of us who are his followers today. This is not another good Bible story to be filed away for small-group discussions later. This is crucial for our lives today!

But let me take the edge off a bit by saying that being a revolutionary, whether on your own or with a group of people, has nothing to do with you and your performance.

Being a revolutionary is simply lifting Jesus up in your life and inviting him to do his revolutionary work in you and through you as you touch others. It has nothing to do with "converting" people to a group, a club, a Church, or a religious system, but it is all about transformation. This is why I've always said that the Reformation never went far enough. We must never settle for anything less than transformation, and the only Person I've ever seen who can accomplish transformation—changing a person's heart inside out—is Jesus.

Consider joining the revolution, because the revolution is still on and thriving all over the planet!

Fellowship: The Key to the Finished Work of Jesus

Jesus' finished work has an additional element that you might overlook. Jesus didn't come just to receive and empower the few disciples God gave him. Jesus came to invite these few individuals into the dynamic of fellowship. Fellowship with Jesus and one another is the key to Jesus' finished work.

Fellowship is best understood as a verb. Fellowship is not an organization, an institution, or a denomination. Fellowship is a verb that, when properly activated, has the power to change the world—one person at a time!

The primary term for fellowship in the New Testament is *koinonia*. The word has the idea of communion or sharing in common with another. It's the perfect word to describe the relationship we are to have with God and with one another—a partnership.

Walking together is practicing the presence of the Kingdom. Practicing the presence of the Kingdom requires fellowship. The term *fellowship* is widely known but even more widely misunderstood. It's more than a potluck dinner. It's not a room called the "fellowship" hall. It's more than a group of friends watching football or hunting together. Fellowship may be the most important concept you will ever learn. However, this concept is not just to be learned; it begs to be lived!

About five years ago, a mutual friend introduced me to a highly successful businessman in Newport Beach over lunch. This man was struggling with several internal problems. He asked if I would meet with him on a regular basis and help him find some answers to his devastating issues.

I said, "No, I can't do that."

He replied, "Oh, I thought that is what you do!"

"Well, I don't like to meet with just one person. It seems to be a more effective experience if there are at least three of us meeting together. Do you have a friend who might join us?"

He said his best friend might join us. Later he called this friend and we began an adventure of getting to know Jesus and getting to know one another for nearly five years. This experience of the power of the few brought solutions, not only to one man's struggles, but to all of us. We met together in the name of Jesus, and Jesus seemed to show up, speaking through our discussions.

Jesus' strategic approach to spreading his good news message throughout the world never involved putting up another Church but practicing church. He taught his followers not to build the Church but to be the church. This is what fellowship is all about!

Fellowship is the answer to becoming the genuine salt and light that Jesus intended his followers to be.[157] My friend who challenged me to be more strategic with my life also painted a couple of vivid pictures that are now etched in my mind indelibly. He urged me to be a fountain. "You don't take the fountain to people; the people come to the fountain," he said. "In the same way, you are to be a light that attracts. Just as bugs are attracted to physical light, people are attracted to spiritual light. So be a light! Be a beacon! If Jesus is lifted up, he will draw all men unto him."

Fellowship operates on the principle of attraction, not promotion. This goes against the grain of most every religious program in our world. But it makes perfect sense within the Kingdom.

The Power of the Few in Your Life

The Kingdom that Jesus intended has to do with experiencing a revolutionary fellowship with Jesus and those who are also following him. Although this isn't the primary purpose of a weekend big-*C* Church service due to the nature of its size, you can experience a revolutionary fellowship within the big-*C* Church in smaller settings. And you can experience it in other opportunities that come your way to gather with other followers of Jesus.

Although I usually meet with two or more men at a time, I did agree to go through the first study book Diana and I wrote, *The Kingdom Secret*, with an individual. Each week, this former Buddhist and I went to lunch.

At the end of a year of this, my friend fell into several horrendous battles in business. He asked me to pray about these matters.

I told him, "We can do better than just my prayer." I urged him to pray before going into each meeting with a bank representative or creditor and ask Jesus for wisdom, then afterward call me and report what wisdom he was given.

Although we prayed for wisdom and were believing for Jesus to come through, we were both shocked that Jesus showed up in a variety of ways in every one of his meetings!

Jesus said that where two or three are gathered together, he will show up.[158] The power of the few is the dwelling place of the presence of Jesus himself. Now, if you were convinced that Jesus was going to show up someplace, wouldn't you go and make yourself available to see him as quickly as possible? Do whatever you can do to participate in the power of the few.

The way to get started is to ask Jesus to show you those you know who might be interested in getting to know Jesus better. Then seek a meeting with those who come to mind, one at a time, and take each person's temperature as to his or her interest in walking together. Even if only one person agrees to come along with you, start with that one!

The power of the few is at the core of what Jesus came to accomplish—to pour his life and energy into those few God sent his way. I hope you will experience this power for yourself. It will change your life, as it changed mine.

CHAPTER 12

When Jesus Shows Up

As I reminded you at the conclusion of the last chapter, Jesus shows up wherever two or three come together in his name.[159] When he does show up, no one is the same again. The dead are brought back to life. The blind see. The lame walk. The deaf hear. The mute talk. Enemies and rivals become friends. The status of women is elevated. The poor are made rich. The rich realize their poverty. The lost are found. The weak find strength. The strong are made aware of weakness.

No transformation is more vivid than what happened to the early disciples. Most were weak willed and timid; they eventually found inner strength and courage. The usual reason given for this dramatic life change is the resurrection of Jesus from the dead. And the resurrection is no doubt paramount. But I see their transformation as coming from something else as well. I see it coming from those forty days after the resurrection when Jesus spoke to the disciples about the Kingdom of God.[160]

Check out what Peter shared regarding that time, when he spoke to those gathered in the house of Cornelius:

We are witnesses of everything he did in the country of the Jews and in Jerusalem. They killed him by hanging him on a cross, but God raised him from the dead on the third day and caused him to be seen. He was not seen by all the people, but by witnesses whom God had already chosen—*by us who ate and drank with him after he rose from the dead.* He commanded us to preach to the people and to testify that he is the one whom God appointed as judge of the living and the dead. All the prophets testify about him that everyone who believes in him receives forgiveness of sins through his name.[161]

I think the real transformation the disciples experienced took place during this time spent with Jesus, eating and drinking and discussing principles of the Kingdom of God.

What if the same thing happens today? When two or three are gathered together in the name of Jesus, he will show up and make a significant difference in all who experience him.

Diana and I have the privilege of gathering together with a few followers of Jesus. We've been meeting with one group of followers weekly for several years. Week after week, as we are doing life together, we have faced nearly every kind of pain, disease, and loss imaginable. We turn every problem over to the care and direction of Jesus. When we need healing, we ask for Jesus to come through on our behalf. When we have financial needs, we ask for his help. When we need wisdom for decision making, we count on his wisdom. When we are grieving a loss of a loved one, we count on his peace. When we seek answers from Jesus, we have found that he shows up.

We have found out that by opening up our lives to one another, most of the answers to our individual prayers are being answered within our group of twenty-two. Even within our discussions, there are so many life-shaping and life-changing takeaways each week.

Here is my point: if Jesus brings positive transformation into every life he encounters, then doesn't it make sense for us to introduce Jesus to everyone who is interested? You see, when Jesus shows up, no one is ever the same again!

Let's take a look at a few of the ways Jesus showed up for people in his day—because this will give us some clues about how he shows up for us.

When Jesus Showed Up for a Sick Woman and a Dead Girl

The Gospels record many stories of Jesus encounters, but two of my favorites show him at his best. We'll be getting to the second—the story of Jesus meeting Zacchaeus in Jericho—shortly. The first is the story of a time when Jesus touched two unclean females, breaking rules, traditions, and customs of the day. This dual miracle took place in the area of Capernaum. Here is the story in total:

> When Jesus had again crossed over by boat to the other side of the lake, a large crowd gathered around him while he was by the lake. Then one of the synagogue leaders, named Jairus, came, and when he saw Jesus, he fell at his feet. He pleaded earnestly with him, "My little daughter is dying. Please come and put your hands on her so that she will be healed and live." So Jesus went with him.

A large crowd followed and pressed around him. And a woman was there who had been subject to bleeding for twelve years. She had suffered a great deal under the care of many doctors and had spent all she had, yet instead of getting better she grew worse. When she heard about Jesus, she came up behind him in the crowd and touched his cloak, because she thought, "If I just touch his clothes, I will be healed." Immediately her bleeding stopped and she felt in her body that she was freed from her suffering.

At once Jesus realized that power had gone out from him. He turned around in the crowd and asked, "Who touched my clothes?"

"You see the people crowding against you," his disciples answered, "and yet you can ask, 'Who touched me?'"

But Jesus kept looking around to see who had done it. Then the woman, knowing what had happened to her, came and fell at his feet and, trembling with fear, told him the whole truth. He said to her, "Daughter, your faith has healed you. Go in peace and be freed from your suffering."

While Jesus was still speaking, some people came from the house of Jairus, the synagogue leader. "Your daughter is dead," they said. "Why bother the teacher anymore?"

Overhearing what they said, Jesus told him, "Don't be afraid; just believe."

He did not let anyone follow him except Peter, James and John the brother of James. When they came to the home of the synagogue leader, Jesus saw a commotion, with people crying and wailing loudly. He went in and said to them, "Why all this commotion and wailing? The child is not dead but asleep." But they laughed at him.

After he put them all out, he took the child's father and mother and the disciples who were with him, and went in where the child was. He took her by the hand and said to her, *"Talitha koum!"* (which means "Little girl, I say to you, get up!"). Immediately the girl stood up and began to walk around (she was twelve years old). At this they were completely astonished. He gave strict orders not to let anyone know about this, and told them to give her something to eat.[162]

This is a fascinating story where Jesus was on his way to perform one miracle and stopped for another divine appointment. These two stories fused together are interesting to compare. Both women are called daughters, one by the father and one by Jesus. Both have to do with the number twelve—the age of Jairus' daughter and the number of years of suffering of the woman. And in both situations faith was key. Jairus and the woman both saw Jesus as the only answer to their need.

A superstition of the time seems to have motivated the woman to touch Jesus' garments. The fringe worn on the border of the outer garment of the Messiah was believed to have special power. If she could just touch that fringe border, then she might be healed of her condition and be able to rejoin society like other women. Whether she believed Jesus was the Messiah or not, she was certainly desperate enough to seek out the power that seemed to be flowing through this new rabbi.

Jesus showed himself to be the physician and healer of the unacceptable and the sick when he healed this woman. Think of her desperation. She had been ceremonially unclean because of her bleeding for twelve years. That adds up to twelve years of disappointment, twelve years of being left out, unable to participate in worship or feasts, twelve years of being rejected and unacceptable, twelve years of feeling like a nobody. She saw Jesus as the only answer she might ever have to solve her problem.

Think what Jesus did for her: Jesus' presence and touch actually healed her. He made her clean—physically, spiritually, and ceremonially. He made her a participant in her community again. He gave her peace. And he made her feel special by not leaving her in the crowd.

No doubt, once Jesus identified her, she must have felt as if she were the only one in the crowd. Jesus didn't let the woman remain as part of the faceless crowd, so he identified her. Jesus actually said, "Be *continually* healed."[163] To the only person he ever called "daughter" in Scripture, he granted continual health in order to reenter society.

After this unusual encounter, Jesus overheard that Jairus' daughter was dead. He interjected himself into the situation, encouraging Jairus, the leader of the Synagogue, not to be afraid and to have faith. It's interesting that Jesus took his three main men along with him as he went to visit the daughter of Jairus who was presumed to be dead. This was another field trip with his disciples, but this time it was a triple-A miracle that was needed at Jairus' house. The girl was dead and the mourners were well into the mourning process. Jesus went into her room and raised her from the dead.

These two women serve as great illustrations of hope when you're in the midst of desperate situations, even to the point of death.

Jesus' encounter with the woman who had been bleeding for twelve years was daring, because in her state of health she was unclean. Then note that while Jesus was busy healing a woman who had been unclean for twelve years, Jairus' twelve-year-old daughter had died. Now Jairus' dead daughter had become unclean through her death.

But no matter, Jesus showed up to touch these two unclean females, bringing instant healing to one and bringing the other back to life.

When Jesus shows up, most often something wonderful happens!

When Jesus Showed Up for Zacchaeus

[Another time,] Jesus entered Jericho and was passing through. A man was there by the name of Zacchaeus; he was a chief tax collector and was wealthy. He wanted to see who Jesus was, but because he was short, he could not see over the crowd. So he ran ahead and climbed a sycamore-fig tree to see him, since Jesus was coming that way.

When Jesus reached the spot, he looked up and said to him, "Zacchaeus, come down immediately. I must stay at your house today." So he came down at once and welcomed him gladly.

All the people saw this and began to mutter, "He has gone to be the guest of a sinner."

But Zacchaeus stood up and said to the Lord, "Look, Lord! Here and now I give half of my possessions to the poor, and if I have cheated anybody out of anything, I will pay back four times the amount."

Jesus said to him, "Today salvation has come to this house, because this man, too, is a son of Abraham. For the

Son of Man came to seek and to save the lost."[164]

For many of us, the story of Jesus' encounter with Zacchaeus is so familiar that we miss the point Jesus was making. I know I did. Let me explain.

Don't miss the context here. Jericho was the main route to take from Galilee to Jerusalem. Jesus had made his way through the city of Jericho from the Galilee area to Jerusalem multiple times, but this was Jesus' last trip through Jericho to Jerusalem. I can imagine that as Jesus' popularity continued to increase, the religious and political leaders of a city like Jericho would expect to welcome him into their city and host him there.

Jesus entered the city, and the city elders, particularly the religious ones, were there to give him their special welcome. Most likely they had plans to socialize with Jesus over a meal. They were the spiritual ones—the righteous—of the city of Jericho.

As they greeted Jesus and walked with him through the city, he changed their plans, offended them, and threatened their super-spiritual position among the people. Jesus essentially turned down their social overtures and picked out one of the lesser ones—Zacchaeus.

Zacchaeus was not viewed among the social elite within Jericho. He wasn't among the religiously accepted, but was an alien of sorts. He was a representation of the sinners within the city—the hated tax collector, maybe even the manager of all of the tax collection in the city.

When Jesus saw Zacchaeus up in the sycamore tree, he noticed him. It's very possible that Jesus already knew Zacchaeus. Jesus possibly addressed him like this: "Zack, come on down. Let's hang out together today—at your house!"

Note that the people who heard this were shocked and not happy! They began to mutter and grumble over the invitation.

I used to believe that when Zacchaeus came down from his perch in the tree and met with Jesus, he confessed his cheating and stealing to Jesus and then Jesus offered him salvation. But this is not what happened!

Zacchaeus didn't have a meeting with Jesus, nor did he confess his cheating and stealing to Jesus. Zacchaeus just landed on his feet at the base of the tree and made his famous statement to Jesus. They had not had any time to talk or discuss his life.

Take a closer look at what Zacchaeus actually said; it changes everything in your interpretation of the scene. Zacchaeus stood up and said to Jesus, "Look, Lord! Here and now I give half of my possessions to the poor, and if I have cheated anybody out of anything, I will pay back four times the amount."[165]

The verbiage is in the present active tense. He is not saying, "Now that I have met you, Jesus, I will give half of what I make to the poor." Rather, he is saying, "Jesus, I am presently giving half of what I own to the poor, and if anyone believes I have cheated them in any way, I am repaying them four times the amount." This shows that Zacchaeus had confidence that he wasn't cheating anyone and was already a charitable man to the poor.

Jesus said to him, "Today salvation has come to this house, because this man, too, is a son of Abraham."[166] I think Jesus set up this divine appointment with Zacchaeus to make a point. Zacchaeus, the man who didn't enjoy religious or super-spiritual status, was far more honest and spiritual than those who held high positions in the city of Jericho. Therefore, this "sinner" possessed salvation and a right standing before God.

Remember, a person's salvation is of the heart and that heart will act out appropriately. Jesus refers to this kind of right standing before God, when he says that only those whose righteousness surpasses—goes beyond, deeper—than the religious leaders with all of their religiosity, will enter the Kingdom of heaven.

Jesus knew Zacchaeus, all right. He knew him well. He knew his heart. The point of this encounter was to clarify who is right before God and who is not. And Jesus loved every moment of it!

When Jesus Showed Up in the Book of Acts

The active presence of Jesus was not limited to the thirty-three years of life he spent from his birth in Bethlehem to his death and resurrection in Jerusalem. In the years recorded in the Book of Acts, Jesus continued to show up among his followers. This is why I like to call this book the Acts of Jesus and not the Acts of the Apostles.

Jesus showed up and the result was his followers sharing Jesus' message of the Kingdom to the world.[167] It was important that his followers knew Jesus personally, so he spent an additional forty days with them with lots of personal interaction. Similarly, it was important that his followers had a strategy for how to take Jesus' message of the Kingdom throughout the world, so Jesus urged them to wait for his Spirit to come upon them and give them the power to spread his revolutionary message to the world.

Jesus showed up through Peter to communicate his message to many nations.[168] Jesus showed up through Peter and John to empower the healing of a lame man.[169] Jesus showed up to empower several articulate moments where his followers were given the most appropriate and powerful things to say.[170] Jesus showed up to redirect Paul to bear his name everywhere—to the house of Israel, to the non-Jewish nations of the world, and to their kings.[171] Jesus showed up to demonstrate to Peter that his message must not be contained within a Jewish box but is for everyone everywhere.[172]

Acts 29—Today!

Several of us who are walking together have found that reading the Acts of Jesus one chapter per day can be an amazing experience. We have read it through for several months at a time, and it increases our own awareness of when and where Jesus is showing up in our lives today.

It's important to note that Jesus' activity didn't stop at the end of the twenty-eighth chapter of Acts. Jesus continues to act each and every day—twenty-four hours a day, 365 days a year. Therefore, we have found it most helpful to move into the rest of our lives with Jesus. We call it Acts 29. It refers to living out our relationship with Jesus today, because Jesus continues to act in and through all followers who have ears to hear and eyes to see.

So today the Acts of Jesus become most evident as one pays attention to the three essentials in following the revolutionary Jesus.

- The preeminence of Jesus, making him first in your life
- The presence of the Kingdom, living it as your lifestyle
- The power of the few, following Jesus with a few like-minded traveling companions

"When and where Jesus shows up" is not just a cliché or hope or mystical experience. It's a reality, and we have been experiencing this reality for several years. In many ways, we see real answers to real prayers—even little things—that, if we were living our lives alone, we would not recognize. To be walking with others and discussing the happenings of life daily greatly assists in being more aware of where and when Jesus shows up. We call them *Jesus sightings*. The Jesus movement was launched when Jesus showed up among his followers—and that transformational movement is still on today!

CHAPTER 13

What It Means to Be a Follower

From the beginning of his earthly ministry, Jesus expressed his most revolutionary call: "Follow me."[173] Then, at the end of his time on earth, Jesus said, "Go and make disciples."[174] A disciple is literally a learner—one who listens to and follows a teacher and his teachings. So, from beginning to end, it's really the same. Jesus invited people to follow him, and he expects his followers to invite others to follow him.

Diana and I, along with our little core group, are doing our best to be faithful followers of Jesus and to introduce him into the many cultures of our world. We see ourselves as simply followers of Jesus, not Christians or believers or Church members. We say it this way among our friends: "We're trying to do the most difficult thing we have ever done in our lives. We're trying to follow the teachings and principles of Jesus." This is discipleship or followership—to know Jesus and to make him known.

A follower of Jesus must make it his or her single-minded focus to be like Jesus as best he can. Simply put, see and hear what Jesus does and do it!

Three Requirements of a Follower

Although there are many and varied lists of what it means to be a Jesus follower, it seems counterproductive to choose a series of characteristics to follow. Here's the problem. Once you have a list, there is a tendency to follow the list and not Jesus.

This is why it's important to find out what Jesus himself said about following him.

As we see in Luke 14, at one point Jesus turned to the many who were following him and challenged them to be his true disciples (followers). He presented three tough requirements to be a genuine follower. Today, these requirements are still tough. But after attempting to live them out, I can say that the benefits far outweigh not doing so.

1. The requirement of priority. Let's join the crowds of people who were walking alongside Jesus for a variety of reasons. "Now as Jesus proceeded on his journey, great crowds accompanied him and he turned and spoke to them, 'If anyone comes to me without hating [setting aside his relationship with] his father and mother and wife and children and brothers and sisters, and even his own life, he cannot be a disciple of mine.'"[175]

There are many reasons people might follow Jesus, but if you want to in fact be a disciple of Jesus, it is necessary to make Jesus number one above all others. He makes it tougher than just saying that he wants to be your best friend after your family members. He requires that you reduce in importance your family members—father, mother, wife, children, brothers, and sisters—in comparison with your relationship with Jesus. He is to be your number-one priority. You go to him first. He makes it even more personal when he says to set aside even your own life.

Jesus wants all who desire to be his disciples to place him above all of our own self-interests. This is the area where we create many of our own little gods that we have come to worship and put ahead of or equal to Jesus. You cannot be full of yourself and be acting as a disciple—a follower of Jesus—at the same time. There is not enough room in your heart for that balancing act.

Then note that Jesus doesn't equivocate at all here. He says that unless you put him as the highest priority in your life—the highest position of authority—"you cannot be my disciple." It's not that you cannot be a good disciple or one of the better disciples or a better than average disciple; it's that you cannot be a disciple of his at all. There is no wiggle room here. Jesus sets the bar very high, even unreachable for many of us at times. Yet Jesus sets up this requirement as a dynamic end game for us to place our single-minded focus upon.

Will you allow me to get personal with you again? So, *do* you want to be a disciple of Jesus? If you do, then make him your number one, above all others. Make him the Person you go to, the one you consult first, and the one you imitate most. The way I see this done is that Jesus wants you to walk with him so closely that you don't start your day, enter into a meeting, begin a conversation, respond to a crisis, react to an enemy, or end your day without talking with him first. This is what it means to make him your priority! Will you take this challenge from Jesus and make him your priority? It doesn't mean to ignore anyone, because we show our love for Jesus in the act of loving others. And you can be sure this is not a call to perfection, but a channeling of your heart's focus.

Our little core group has been practicing something for years that seems to be most helpful in keeping Jesus as our priority. We work to be diligent in advancing the conversation of Jesus every day in all circumstances. We are learning that advancing the conversation of Jesus begins with listening—listening to Jesus personally, listening to Jesus as he speaks through others, and listening to see what Jesus is up to today. By the way, when you are looking for a Jesus sighting, remember that Jesus rarely shows up by appointment. Most of the time Jesus shows up as an irritation to our schedules.

2. The requirement of perseverance. The second prerequisite to being one of Jesus' disciples is to make him your priority no matter what happens to you! Your relationship with Jesus is your highest priority and you will not be deterred from following him and shaping your life after him by anything. You will hang in there no matter what—no matter the troubles you face or the stress that arises because of your association with Jesus.

Here's how Jesus states this requirement: "And whoever does not carry their cross and follow me cannot be my disciple."[176] Jesus' disciple must carry the cross just as Jesus did—following in the footsteps of Jesus. If you are unwilling to do this, then you cannot be his disciple.

So, what does Jesus mean by "carry his cross"?

The cross of Jesus was the greatest expression of sacrificial love ever. Here is God's Messiah—the most powerful Person ever born—and his ultimate act was a demonstration of love, not power. The Roman Empire's symbol was the cross—an emblem of domination and power—because of their method of discipline, crucifixion. Jesus turned this symbol of cruelty and power into the ultimate symbol of sacrificial love.

Jesus' plan was to demonstrate the love of God to the world by allowing himself to die on that Roman cross—transforming the terrifying symbol of the cross into a symbol of hope, peace, and grace. Now, that's the greatest example of sacrificial love ever, and it triggered the Jesus movement that has transformed more lives and cultures than any other movement in all history.

For us, carrying Jesus' cross has to do with identifying our mission in life so much with Jesus that we actually incarnate him, or flesh him out. Carrying our cross is to be a sacrificial lover—to be Jesus in all we say and do. The experience of the cross was one of shame and degradation. Carrying Jesus' cross requires the perseverance to follow Jesus, even when faced with that same kind of shame and degradation.

Normally, when Jesus talked about the cross and discipleship, he used the term to "take up" the cross. Luke uses a different word here—the word that means to carry or bear the cross, as opposed to taking up or picking up the cross. The term Luke uses refers, not literally to carry something, but to having something attached to you. It's the same term Acts uses when it talks about Paul's mission to bear the name of Jesus to the Gentiles, to their kings, and to the house of Israel. The root word means to walk with or carry the name of Jesus—to be so identified with Jesus' name that he was not only Paul's partner but his identity.[177]

Paul didn't have to pick up the cross; he was already attached to Jesus. When you carry the cross, you are so identified with Jesus that you are to be Jesus to the world around you. It's to be proactive with the love of Jesus rather than reactive against whatever or whoever assaults you.

There is a cost in carrying your cross. Following Jesus as your highest priority and fleshing him out in your life will stir up lots of controversy.

When you take the path of Jesus versus the normal ways of religious living, you may suffer some negative consequences. Choosing the sacrificial love approach will most certainly separate you from most religious people, because you are like Jesus, a contrarian, going against the religious grain.

A sad thing happened as the Church of Jesus became organized: the cross took on that same idea of domination and power it originally had. The organized Church of Christendom took on the power of being the only channel for salvation and communication with God. From the Roman Empire to Jesus to organized Christianity, the symbol of the cross went full circle. To carry the cross of Jesus in his footsteps is to resist this domination and power motif and to reverse the momentum back to the sacrificial love of Jesus. You may find great resistance as you take on this lifestyle.

Another consequence of carrying your cross is that you must endure everything that is thrown at you—trials, troubles, stresses, injustices, and all kinds of things that will require you to give of yourself in a sacrificial way. When you think you can't take it any longer, you still hang on. It's the requirement of perseverance—hanging in there with Jesus no matter what!

As Diana and I have learned to follow Jesus more closely, we are amazed at what opportunities and oppositions come our way. More and more is asked of us as we walk this walk. Again, this is why I say, "This is the toughest thing I've ever tried to do—to follow the teachings and principles of Jesus."

Basketball coaches say to players, "Don't feel the pressure to go out on the floor and make things happen; let the game come to you." This is how we are learning to persevere in following Jesus. Instead of initiating everything ourselves, we are constantly preparing our hearts and waiting for life to unfold. We are then ready to respond to it.

This is even more important when the circumstances of our lives are not going well. The only thing you can change is yourself and how you respond to life's circumstances. Keep in mind that it's not what happens to you but how you handle what happens that counts most.

3. The requirement of properly possessing your possessions. This final requirement may be the toughest of all. Before he actually presented it, Jesus offered two illustrations that strongly urge you to count the cost of what it means to follow Jesus.

The first has to do with the building of a tower: "If any of you wanted to build a tower, wouldn't he first sit down and work out the cost of it, to see if he can afford to finish it? Otherwise, when he has laid the foundation and found himself unable to complete the building, everyone who sees it will begin to jeer at him, saying, 'This is the man who started to build a tower but couldn't finish it!'"[178]

Then Jesus illustrated counting the cost with a king going off to war against another king: "Or, suppose there is a king who is going to war with another king, doesn't he sit down first and consider whether he can engage the twenty thousand of the other king with his own ten thousand? And if he decides he can't, then while the other king is still a long way off, he sends messengers to him to ask for conditions of peace."[179]

Finally Jesus revealed his third requirement: "So it is with you; only the man who says goodbye to all his possessions can be my disciple."[180] Or to put it another way: "In the same way, those of you who do not give up everything you have cannot be my disciples."[181] Naturally, the wording "give up everything" is the operative phrase here. What does it mean to give up everything?

The Greek word here means to "take leave of" or "renounce" your possessions. Jesus is not saying that you are to give over all your possessions, but to give them up—to renounce ownership of all you have. You really *don't* own what you have. You are a manager or steward of what God has allowed you to collect. Jesus wants you to realize this and be willing to give up your personal ownership of all you have for Jesus and the Kingdom. Jesus wants you to hold on to your stuff, but hold it loosely and be ready to share generously as it is needed. It's really giving up your dependence on it and depending on Jesus instead.

It's even more than this. You are not just to give up everything you have but to give up all you are as well—your very existence! This is inherent in the word used for possessions. Jesus owns it all—you and all of your stuff. The call, then, is to learn to wear the cloak of materialism loosely and to live your life as one who is owned and directed by Jesus. The truth is, when you die, all that is left is a big (or a little) garage sale to handle your stuff. Live for something more than that.

When Diana and I began our walk with Jesus we determined that we are managers of what we have and that it all belongs to Jesus. When you live under the teaching of the tithe, you get to thinking that all God wants is a portion of you and your stuff. We are now convinced that he wants it all made available for his use in his way and in his time. This was our surrender to Jesus as our Master, and we are satisfied this is the most enjoyable and satisfying way to live our lives.

In the Spirit of Surrender

Make Jesus your highest priority over all relationships; make him your priority no matter what; and renounce the ownership of all you are and have. These are three requirements of being a disciple of Jesus.

The spirit of these discipleship requirements is all about surrender— abandoning all competing relationships and securities for Jesus and the Kingdom. There are many examples of surrender, and it isn't the same for all. Peter, James, and John left their fishing business to follow Jesus full time. Levi also left his position at the local tax collections office. Zacchaeus did not leave his vocation, but he did give half his fortune to the poor. There is the rich young ruler who was unwilling to renounce his wealth and follow Jesus; he walked away with great sadness. Paul, from the book of Acts, didn't leave his profession of making tents; he was able to take his profession with him wherever he went.

Diana and I are devoting ourselves to practicing these three very tough requirements of Jesus. What's interesting is that the more closely you follow alongside Jesus, the easier it is to live as a disciple. Living like this has been a graduate-school experience of how to walk with Jesus, walk with others, and to wait on Jesus to lead out with orders and opportunities. I urge you to accept the same kind of education.

CHAPTER 14

Making Jesus a Habit

I want to share with you three vital habits we practice in following Jesus. These habits not only summarize what we have learned in following Jesus; they will give you several new handles on how to follow Jesus in your world.

Now, let me say right away that it's not my intention to offer you list after list of things you *must* do in order to follow Jesus. Most of my life, while teaching and preaching, I gave three steps to do this or five steps to do that. If I did this on a weekly basis as I had done it for over twenty-five years, the list would be quite a pile of things to do! Where can anyone find the time to apply these lists, even if they were the truth? That approach said, "Follow Jesus Tim's way." Not anymore!

My purpose is to share with you what Jesus said and did, along with my personal experience with a few traveling companions. That's all.

Let me illustrate the approach in this way. Three pastors from a local megachurch asked me to meet with them. I agreed, and they posed a fascinating question: "How can we, as pastors, follow Jesus?" This perceptive question came as quite a shock to me. I loved it!

My response was immediate. I said, "I have absolutely no idea how you can follow Jesus as pastors, but I am willing to walk through this question with you. I have no doubt that you can figure it out as we walk together." We did, and they did!

This chapter is that kind of sharing. As a simple and stubborn follower of Jesus, I have found that it's vital to embrace three basic habits for myself.

Habit 1: Walking with Jesus

Walking with Jesus means you are devoted to Jesus.

- *Devoted to imitate Jesus*—to walk, talk, love, and think like Jesus. The question to check this is "What did Jesus do?" (WDJD?). Follow him.

- *Devoted to consult with Jesus* regarding your personal, family, and professional decisions. The question to check this is "What would Jesus do?" (WWJD?).

- *Devoted to converse with Jesus* throughout your day. Prayer is simply a conversation within your relationship with Jesus. The question to check this is "What is Jesus saying?" (WIJS?).

- *Devoted to community the way Jesus was*—disciplining yourself to do life with a few others. The question to check this is "What is Jesus doing?" (WIJD?).

On every airplane a flight attendant gives the instruction "Put your oxygen mask on first and then help those around you." Walking with Jesus is just like that. Put on your oxygen mask—your personal relationship with Jesus. That's what comes first—always!

Walking with Jesus is being aware of his constant presence in your life. It's being with him, hanging out with him in constant dependence on his strength and his lead. Walking with Jesus is learning to count on him in your everyday life. In simple terms, do what he says. No matter what he says to do and say, you just do it. I heard it in a funny way several years ago: "If you pray for a Cadillac and God sends a jackass, ride it." It's signing off as king of your kingdom and making Jesus the King of all kings. To walk with Jesus is to be willing to let him direct your life.

Habit 2: Walking with Others

As always, Jesus is our example of this habit. When he began his ministry, he chose three to come alongside him—to be with him. He continued to spend most of his time with these three. This small group expanded to twelve, then the seventy-two, and then the 120. In fact, at one point there were up to five hundred who were fairly close disciples of Jesus. I'm sure most everyone who followed Jesus felt close to him, yet he walked mostly with a few.

Jesus also sent his early disciples out in pairs, not alone, and then the early disciples continued to follow Jesus' example. They continued to model this by spending time together, studying the teachings of Jesus, eating, praying, and fellowshipping with one another.

Walking with others provides a level of personal support that we all need. Walking with others provides strength to handle whatever may come in life. There's something about knowing you are not alone that empowers. Without others in your life, you are weakened and at your lowest. Encouragement is easily drained, yet you will find yourself fueled by the others who are doing life with you. Without others, you can easily become distracted, even discouraged.

Diana and I continue to experience this empowerment as we walk with a few. We just don't act on our own any longer. We seek the counsel of our small group and act—travel, teach, and write—with their blessing and support. This family of Jesus followers who are committing to do life with us know they are invited to offer any and all counsel, including, if necessary, confrontation. We now do everything in the strength and affirmation of our dear friends. This is not a one-way street. We feel the same freedom to speak into their lives.

A learning dynamic presents itself within a smaller setting. When walking with others, it's so much easier to experience how others are living the principles of Jesus. When you walk with others, your own seeing and hearing seem to be better. If you want ears to hear and eyes to see Jesus, operate within a group.

Finally and most importantly, walking with others is a sure place where Jesus will show up. Without others you tend to forget how real and present Jesus is. Walking with others is one of those disciplines of life that produces great results for you and those with whom you are walking.

Living fully requires that you walk with Jesus. When you walk with him, you are the walking solution to people's needs everywhere. And the only way to faithfully walk with Jesus is to walk together.

Paul was a master at including others. He must have been a southerner, because he used what I call the *y'all principle* throughout most of his writing. He did this by using the plural form of "you." Take a look:

- "Let the word of Christ richly dwell within you [among y'all], with all wisdom teaching and admonishing one another with psalms and hymns and spiritual songs, singing with thankfulness in your hearts to God."[182]

• "I am again in labor until Christ is formed in you [in y'all]."[183]

• "Christ in you [in y'all], the hope of glory."[184]

Paul was commanding believers everywhere to allow Jesus to make his dwelling place (make himself at home) with them as they come together in fellowship. The power of the gospel will be present in the midst of a few who are gathered together in Jesus' name. The y'all principle is the fellowship principle and the practice of the presence of the Kingdom.

It is amazing how simple agreements and commitments to one another provide a bonding power among the participants. These covenants may be agreements to pray for certain things for a certain time period, going on a trip together, producing an event, or agreements to go through a study together.

This is the fellowship principle. God is calling you into the fellowship of Jesus and his people.

Habit 3: Waiting on Jesus to Lead Out

It's not only waiting on Jesus to lead out, but waiting on Jesus to lead out with orders and opportunities. Learning this habit and really getting it was the toughest for me. This requires the discipline of trust. And, as if that weren't enough, I've learned you must let go of the results and turn them over to Jesus, too.

Waiting on Jesus to lead out with orders and opportunities is tough, because you are no longer in charge of what's happening and when it's going to happen. You are forced to let it go, since you are not in charge. All along you thought you were in charge of your life, but you are not!

• As you practice waiting, there is the *action of readying yourself.* Your responsibility is not to be in charge but to be ready for the King's orders.

- As you practice waiting, there is the *action of relating to Jesus and to others*—the first two habits. Your responsibility is to continue these relationships within your support team, the "one anothers" in your life. It's the doing of life together, not sitting around and explaining it.

- As you practice waiting, there is the *action of resting*. Your responsibility is to be anxious for nothing and to rest in your relationship with Jesus and with others.

Now, keep in mind that Jesus may not have direct orders for you today. Don't be in a hurry to the point of being stressed. Following Jesus is all about rest. Jesus calls his disciples into his rest—confident, peaceful, everything-is-going-to-be-okay rest.

We *are* waiting for Jesus to show up in our lives. We *are* waiting for Jesus to give us answers to our heart's cry—an impression, a peace, a desire, or a thought. We *are* to wait to bring restoration to those God brings us. We *are* to wait for God to bring people into our lives for us to walk with in fellowship and support.

Waiting on Jesus to lead out is demonstrating a ruthless trust in him to come through on our behalf with opportunities and orders for us to follow.

One Day at a Time

Jesus said, "Do not worry about tomorrow, for tomorrow will worry about itself. Each day has enough trouble of its own."[185]

I've said it many times:

Yesterday is a cancelled check.

Tomorrow is a promissory note.

Today is the only cash you have.

Alcoholics Anonymous and all of the other Anonymous groups operate upon the theme of "one day at a time." This is exactly what Jesus is saying here—one day at a time. Worry has little to do with the past; it mostly has to do with the future. We worry over what might happen or what might not happen. It's not in our control, but we spend lots of energy as if our worry could make a difference in the outcome. Jesus says, "Don't bother!" Each day has plenty of trouble of its own without our worrying about tomorrow.

Jesus teaches that if you are seeking his Kingdom and his righteousness, he will take care of everything else you need.[186] He will do this one day at a time. This is what God did with the children of Israel about one month into their forty years of wandering. He rained down bread from heaven—manna—each day, except on the Sabbath. Each day the manna came down from heaven. Each day they were to gather enough for the day, never thinking of storing up some for tomorrow. Each day there was enough.[187]

Jesus is the new manna in town. Jesus is our daily bread. The word "manna" means a surprise, like "What is it?" I see Jesus giving each of us a surprise of his manna, his leadership, his sustenance each and every day as we seek first his Kingdom and his righteousness. We practice these habits in order to gather the manna for today, which helps in minimizing our worry factor.

Have you noticed that when you think about tomorrow or next week, the worries become overwhelming? I have to constantly focus my thinking and reflection upon today.

This goes along with the message of the book of Ecclesiastes. King Solomon had tried everything to fill his life with satisfaction and all was found to be empty—luxury, liquor, lust. But at the end of the book he sums up his life's search with two summary truths.

1. Fear God and keep His commandments.[188]

2. Enjoy your blessings every day.[189]

Paul would say the same thing, but in different terminology. It's all about "the simplicity and purity of devotion to Christ."[190] And that simplicity and purity of devotion is found in these three habits:

- walking with Jesus
- walking with others
- waiting on Jesus to lead out with orders and opportunities

Do all of these one day at a time.

CHAPTER 15

Showing Off Jesus

The vice president of marketing for a dog-food company stood before his national sales force to give them a rah-rah session.

"Who has the best dog food in the nation?" he called out.

"We do!" they replied.

"Who has the best marketing program in the USA?"

"We do!"

"Who has the best packaging and pricing?"

"We do!"

The VP's voice took on a more sober tone. "Then why is it that out of nineteen dog-food companies in the country we are number nineteen?"

No one said a word as everyone fidgeted and squirmed. Then one brave soul in the back whimpered out an answer: "Because dogs don't like it."

This is the problem we face around the world with the message of Jesus. Jesus has been so enmeshed with Christianity and religiosity that people just don't like it.

So, as followers of Jesus, how can we best show Jesus off? How can we best lift Jesus up so people can see him without religious blinders? How can we advance the conversation of Jesus most effectively?

Five Ways to Show Jesus Off

Jesus said that many are interested in him, even interested enough to follow him.[191] We're looking for those who are interested. This is really the only requirement that is necessary—to be interested. Disciples of Jesus orbit around their world, looking for those who have ears to hear and eyes to see. You're not looking to close any spiritual deals or for people to preach to; you're looking for the interested. They are all around you.

Years ago *The Last Temptation of Christ* movie was released. At best, it was a bad movie and probably would not have lasted more than a couple of weeks in the theaters, but it was actually promoted by Christians. Because Christians organized against this movie with signs and angry demonstrations, they drew massive media attention, which in turn attracted more people into the theaters to see the movie.

I learned a great lesson through that experience. Jesus doesn't need or want demonstrations *for* him. Jesus wants his followers to be demonstrations *of* him—doing what Jesus would do and saying what he would say.

In order to demonstrate Jesus in your world, it's important to be like Jesus in all of your actions. As I've combed through the teachings of Jesus, I have discovered five specific ways to demonstrate him—to show Jesus off.

1. How you live your life. Jesus said, "You are the light of the world. A town built on a hill cannot be hidden. Neither do people light a lamp and put it under a bowl. Instead they put it on its stand, and it gives light to everyone in the house. In the same way, let your light shine before others, that they may see your good deeds and glorify your Father in heaven."[192]

By this we see that it is possible for people to be attracted to God through your good deeds—your lifestyle. How you live your life speaks loudly to those who are watching. How you handle your problems and stresses, how you love your spouse, and how you treat your family and friends are all on display. People can see Jesus in this way!

Note that there are no words spoken by you here. It's not the fancy or spiritual talk but the walk that matters most to people. People watch closely for that ethos—that credibility in your life. When they see it in your actions, then (and only then) your words have weight.

Diana and I are always getting feedback that we and our friends are so different. It's not what we do so much as it is what we don't do. We don't enter into gossip. We don't condemn others. We don't act like we have it all together. We don't cover up our weaknesses and mistakes. We love both the powerful and the poor. We embrace the disenfranchised. We don't hesitate to serve when asked. This kind of down-to-earth, authentic lifestyle is so attractive. This kind of lifestyle is Jesus!

2. How you treat others. Jesus said, "A new command I give you: Love one another. As I have loved you, so you must love one another. By this everyone will know that you are my disciples, if you love one another."[193]

People see Jesus by our love for one another. This is so attractive and contagious. People all around you are desperate to love and be loved. Remember what I said earlier: we are not in need of more love in the world, but more lovers.

Jesus is reflected in this kind of love for one another. Jesus is not reflected in the divisiveness of the many religious communities that seem to compete and war against one another. It's ugly and it's devoid of the sacrificial love message Jesus came to bring. Jesus prayed that all those who follow him might be one—in unity with him. Jesus unites; all else divides.

We just returned from the National Prayer Breakfast in Washington, DC. Every year we take new people along with us so they can experience the wonder of representatives coming from over 160 nations to pray together in the spirit of Jesus. This year we took a neighbor whose response this morning (five days later) was that she still is feeling the love she experienced among the people from the ends of the earth and those who were in our group. That love is Jesus lived out among his people!

3. *How you respond to attacks.* Consider these words from Peter, rooted in the ethics of the one who taught us to love our enemies.[194]

All of you, be like-minded, be sympathetic, love one another, be compassionate and humble. Do not repay evil with evil or insult with insult. On the contrary, repay evil with blessing, because to this you were called so that you may inherit a blessing. For,

"Whoever would love life
 and see good days
must keep their tongue from evil
 and their lips from deceitful speech.
They must turn from evil and do good;
 they must seek peace and pursue it.
For the eyes of the Lord are on the righteous
 and his ears are attentive to their prayer,
but the face of the Lord is against those who do evil."

> Always be prepared to give an answer to everyone who asks
> you to give the reason for the hope that you have.[195]

People who give a blessing when insulted are acting in a counter-cultural way. It's moving to the beat of a different drummer in the name and spirit of Jesus.

When you bless someone who insults you, then people notice that you live your life differently from most everyone else who wants to get ahead or who wants to get even. Note that when you act this way, those watching will often ask you for the reason for your rare response to the insults sent your way. This is a perfect time to share with those who ask about the Jesus way of life.

It's impossible to be in leadership and not get a little stabbing in the back. I learned quickly that I must work on forgiving others as soon as possible in order to experience true freedom. My kids always wanted me to get even with these "bad guys" and put them in their places. We played a little game as a family. I read to them what Paul said about how to treat your enemy:

> If your enemy is hungry, feed him;
> > if he is thirsty, give him something to drink.
> In doing this, you will heap burning coals on his head.[196]

From that time on, whenever we had a chance to do something good to one of our enemies, we all high-fived one another and laughed about the burning heads of our enemies.

My kids have grown up knowing the power of blessing those who curse you. Now, as we all follow the teachings of Jesus, we see it differently. Jesus takes it a little further and actually teaches how to wipe out our enemies altogether. Jesus says, "Love them!"

4. *What you tell others.* The apostle Paul wrote, "How can people call for help if they don't know who to trust? And how can they know who to trust if they haven't heard of the One who can be trusted? And how can they hear if nobody tells them? And how is anyone going to tell them, unless someone is sent to do it?"[197]

Using words—this too is one of the ways we show Jesus off, though only one. Note that this is not you preaching to or arguing with anyone. The best thing to share is your own personal story. No one can argue with your own experience and the hope you have found through knowing and following Jesus. This book is an example of my sharing my personal journey of Jesus apprehending me. Don't be afraid to share *your* story. When you are a follower of Jesus, your story is really Jesus' story through you!

Jesus sent out his early followers without giving them a set speech or presentation. He took an entirely different approach. He promised them that they would be given what to say by his Spirit (Matthew 10:19–20). So quit talking so much and start embracing Jesus as a lifestyle, learning how to love one another, and then he will give you what to say when you need it.

As I said earlier, this happened to me when speaking at the Dalai Lama event. I was one of fourteen speakers set to speak to more than 750 clerics from all religions. I was scared. I had no idea what to say. All that I had thought about saying beforehand now seemed inappropriate. It wasn't until I was introduced that it came to me.

I was amazed at what came out of my mouth! I said, "I bring you greetings in the name of Jesus. It's only right that Jesus be among us, because Jesus is all inclusive. He'll work with anyone. He has no system of dos and don'ts for us to do or else. And Jesus is not owned by Christianity or any Christian."

What was so amazing to me is that I had never said any of those things until I was standing before the Dalai Lama and his religious friends from all over the world. I was amazed; my friends were amazed; and the people listening were amazed. All of us were freshly attracted to Jesus. It was beautiful!

5. *How you take care of the needy.* In Jesus' story about the sheep and the goats, the king welcomes the righteous into his Kingdom and commends them for taking care of him when he was needy. This seems to mystify these people. "Lord," they ask, "when did we see You hungry, and feed You, or thirsty, and give You something to drink? And when did we see You a stranger, and invite You in, or naked, and clothe You? When did we see You sick, or in prison, and come to You?"[198]

To this the King answers, "Truly I say to you, to the extent that you did it to one of these brothers of Mine, even the least of them, you did it to Me."[199]

Here Jesus reveals another way that will have a most definite impact in the world and demonstrate the heart of Jesus. Here the sacrificial love message of Jesus is spread by being aware of Jesus' heart and recognizing that Jesus can be found in those in need in our world—the hungry, the thirsty, the naked, the stranger, the sick, and those in prison.

Once a month, a group of us feed and minister to the needs of the homeless in Orange County. I always encourage each of the volunteers by saying that by loving and ministering to these dear people, they are actually ministering to Jesus himself.

Jesus also spoke directly to those who didn't notice him in the midst of the needy. The king in the story says to the wicked, "Truly I tell you, whatever you did not do for one of the least of these, you did not do for me."[200] When we are aware of the poor and needy around us, we are demonstrating the heart of Jesus in our world. Jesus always sought them out, and so should we. When we do, the attractiveness of the sacrificial love of Jesus shines through. Again, there is no talking required here.

When members of our little group were going regularly to feed the homeless, we made it a point to invite our friends to come along. What they found was one of the richest experiences ever. They were able to interact with a homeless person and discover the real story behind the rags and bags. And when a person returned to help the homeless, the homeless remembered them. That becomes addicting! We used this field trip experience to teach what is on the heart of Jesus. Many who came along with us were members of some religious organization—Churches, mosques, temples. The Jesus friendships that were initially developed in serving the homeless are still very much alive today!

Divine Appointments

Each of these actions shows Jesus off to the world—living a lifestyle like Jesus, loving one another, blessing when insulted, sharing your own story, and helping those in need. In fact, when you do these things, you are living life on a different level altogether, and people notice. The people who notice are all of the people who are watching you day after day. This is Kingdom living at its core!

Every morning when I wake up, I say, "Good morning, Jesus! What do you have for me to do today?" With this greeting and question, I set out on a most amazing adventure—every day! Like everyone else, I have all kinds of appointments throughout my day. However, I am looking to see where Jesus might show up, whether in a scheduled appointment (where I know who I'm meeting and when it is), a spontaneous appointment (where I know the person but hadn't planned on seeing him today), or a surprise appointment (where I don't know the person and had no idea I might meet him).

Just today, I was writing this chapter in a local restaurant, when I had a spontaneous appointment with an old friend and his wife. They don't live here. I haven't seen them for over twenty years. We noticed one another at the same time and immediately embraced. They were such an encouragement to me as he expressed their love for me and reminded me twice that we are friends. Then, as I left the restaurant later, my friend walked me outside and said, "I believe this was an appointment set up by God for us to run into one another." There was no doubt in my mind!

I believe God is setting up divine appointments all day long just for you. He wants to love and touch people through you. All he wants from you is for you to show up.

Show up, and you'll be showing Jesus off at the same time.

CHAPTER 16

Your End Game

My wife and I recently participated in a 9/11 event at southern California's Mariners Church, where the Muslim/Christian divide was addressed by several speakers and a series of table discussions.

At our first table discussion, one of the pastors from Mariners asked, "Tim, what would you say to Christians about relating to Muslims?"

I answered, "I believe Christians have the wrong end game as they approach Muslims. Christians have the end game of luring, persuading, and even converting Muslims in order to make them Christians. Making Muslims Christians only deepens the great division between them."

I continued, "Why would you *want* to make a Muslim a Christian?"

I've engaged in this conversation on lots of occasions. The usual response to me is a thoughtful nodding of the head, then silence.

Last year, when Diana and I were in Bethlehem, we caught up with one of the superstars of Christianity, who was speaking at a Palestinian Christian conference. This teacher was the first to ever share with me how easy it was to teach the Bible in Muslim mosques around the world.

Then he asked, "What are you doing now?"

I told him we are doing our best to follow Jesus personally and to introduce Jesus into the many cultures of the world.

He quickly replied, "Yes, we must do our best to bring them into Christianity." He was on his way to Gaza to spend time with his Muslim friends with the end game of somehow, someway, someday making them Christians.

Instead of arguing with a much older Christian icon, I kept reframing his words to mean introducing them to Jesus.

Several years ago, a friend of mine was visiting people in northern India. By that time, my friend had learned what it means to live out the principles of Jesus—to avoid any and all conversion tactics and to focus on advancing the conversation of Jesus. He made a new friend in India who was a missionary to the Hindus. The mission work was not going well, unless his goal was to suffer persecution, death threats, and cultural oppression.

My friend introduced this missionary to the principles I present in *Simply Enough*. The missionary "got it" right away. He quickly understood why he was suffering so much, with very few finding Jesus. His end game was all about converting Hindus into Christians. When he changed his approach, his work among the Hindus became more effective. You see, before, he had the wrong end game, and it didn't work!

Church leaders are becoming more and more concerned over why so many Churches are shutting down in the United States today. For the most part, Churches aren't experiencing genuine new growth. Instead, most megachurches grow through people transferring from other Churches. Honest leaders know this is true, and therefore they look for new ways to reach out to new prospects.

A pastor of one of the local megachurches asked me to advise him on how to reach out to the many ethnic cultures in the area.

I asked him two questions. First, "Is your goal to bring them into your Church?" Second, "Is your goal to make them Christians?"

He answered "Yes!" to both.

I was afraid of that.

I told him what I'll tell you: if getting others to come to Church or become Christians is your end game, you will almost certainly turn away the very people you are hoping to attract.

At a recent President's National Prayer Breakfast, I had the privilege of speaking at one of the regional dinners. My topic was "What's Your End Game?" Afterward, a Pakistani introduced himself to me, saying, "I am a Christian who plants Churches in Pakistan."

Shocked, I said, "Really! How is that working for you?"

He said, "Not well. We are threatened and persecuted continually! We fear for our lives and for the lives of those who convert to Christianity."

(How true this was! Tragically, the Christian cabinet-member friend who was standing with him as we talked was assassinated three weeks later upon his return to Pakistan. He was a marked man because of his faith and because of the threat that Christianity is perceived to be within his Muslim nation.)

My new acquaintance continued, "Through your talk tonight, I see we have the wrong end game. We need to introduce Pakistanis to Jesus and stop trying to convert them to Christianity." That was the most satisfying experience after speaking that I've had in years! This pastor not only listened; he really got it.

———————————————

Please listen carefully to this statement: *Unless Jesus is your end game, then your life amounts to nothing.* Jesus said it himself: "Apart from me you can do nothing."[201] The apostle Paul agreed, saying that his entire life and his accomplishments were a pile of rubbish (actually manure) compared to knowing Jesus.[202] Without Jesus as *your* end game, your life will be filled with frustrations in your religious experience. You will have disappointments with life's expectations, anxiety over whether your children will follow in your religious traditions, concern over the lifestyle decisions of your children and grandchildren, fears for your future security, terror over immediate financial concerns, and discouragement with life's results.

These are not just theoretical experiences, but they have been our experiences without Jesus as *our* end game! Now that Jesus is our life's end game, all of these worries and concerns take on a different perspective altogether. We have found Jesus, simply Jesus, more than adequate in every way. This is not a religious experience but a personal one.

Making Jesus your end game initiates the process of stripping away all add-ons and totally devoting your life, loved ones, and livelihood to Jesus plus nothing else. To make Christ your end game will not work! Jesus warned us, "Many will come . . . claiming, 'I am the Christ.'"[203] To make your religion your end game will not work! There are many religions! To make your Church your end game will not work! To make your religious traditions your end game will not work! Jesus—the Name above all names and the Person above all persons—is the only end game that matters. You may say this is just semantics, but it isn't. This is personal. His name is Jesus!

Insights on the End Game

Jesus made it clear in his teachings that he is the only end game necessary. Let's look at just three examples and what they teach us.

The religious leaders and the Scriptures. Jesus said to the religious leaders, "You study the Scriptures diligently because you think that in them you have eternal life. These are the very Scriptures that testify about *me*, yet you refuse to come to *me* to have life."[204]

Even something as wonderful as the Scriptures is not to become our end game. Jesus is to be our end game.

Peter curious about John's fate. At the breakfast meeting Jesus had with his disciples after the resurrection, an intriguing conversation occurred. Jesus said to Peter:

> "When you were younger you dressed yourself and went where you wanted; but when you are old you will stretch out your hands, and someone else will dress you and lead you where you do not want to go." Jesus said this to indicate the kind of death by which Peter would glorify God. Then he said to him, "Follow *me!*"
>
> [Peter turned and saw that John was following them.] When Peter saw him, he asked, "Lord, what about him?"
>
> Jesus answered, "If I want him to remain alive until I return, what is that to you? You must follow *me*."[205]

We're not to make it our business how Jesus relates to anyone else. We're to make it our business to relate to Jesus personally—making him our end game.

Witnesses in the Spirit. Before Jesus' ascension into heaven, he directed his disciples to wait in Jerusalem. Jesus said, "You will receive power when the Holy Spirit comes on you; and you will be *my* witnesses in Jerusalem, and in all Judea and Samaria, and to the ends of the earth."[206]

Our end game should not be to bear witness to our particular religious persuasion. It should not be to bear witness to our local religious affiliation. It should not be to bear witness to our cultural distinctives. Our end game is to be Jesus (represent Jesus), and bear witness to him.

How to Hear the Shepherd's Voice

By now, I hope you're determined to make Jesus your end game. But you might be asking the obvious question: *How?* Well, it's a matter of following him—Jesus, simply Jesus. And to follow him, you must first hear his voice.

Jesus said, "I am the good shepherd; I know my sheep and my sheep know *me*. . . . I have other sheep that are not of this sheep pen. I must bring them also. They too will listen to *my* voice, and there shall be one flock and one shepherd."[207] So there it is: You can get the guidance you really need from Jesus, the shepherd.

This guidance can only be found in your day-to-day relationship with Jesus. You can get to know him, and know what he wants, by talking with him daily and often. Sometimes we would rather have a good Scripture verse or rule to follow. At times this seems easier, but Jesus doesn't want it this way. He wants you to stop and listen. Why would Jesus say you can listen to his voice if it weren't true? Are you listening to his voice?

So, how do you hear the voice of Jesus? Let me offer five basics to prepare you for hearing the voice of Jesus:

1. Immerse yourself in the Scriptures. Read, reread, and meditate on the Scriptures as you would a love letter, not a research paper. Always search for Jesus wherever you are reading, not getting sidetracked with anything else. Make Jesus your primary lens as you read through the Scriptures. Remember, it's the spirit of the law, not the letter of the law, that matters. Focusing on the letter of the law was the mistake the religious leaders who confronted Jesus made, and he was continually correcting them. They were so wrapped up in Bible memory and organizing the Scriptures into doctrinal systems that they missed Jesus in the process. Jesus can be seen throughout these Scriptures.

When Jesus was working with his disciples, the Scriptures that existed were three groups of books: the Law, or Torah; the Writings, which included Proverbs and Psalms; and then the Prophets. That's why it's so fascinating to see what happened when Jesus was walking with two disciples on the road to Emmaus. He said to them, "This is what I told you while I was still with you: Everything must be fulfilled that is written about me in the Law of Moses, the Prophets and the Psalms." Then he opened their minds so they could understand the Scriptures. [208] Jesus walked them through the Law, the Prophets, and the Psalms in order to open their minds about himself. He was present in every part of the Scriptures.

The entire Bible speaks of Jesus. Listen to him there.

2. Be aware of the Jesus themes throughout the Scriptures. You may not find direct mentions of Jesus everywhere you look in the Scriptures. But you can find the *themes* he cares about everywhere.

For instance, there is the theme of the Shekinah glory—the visible presence of God—throughout Scripture. Beginning with the presence of God in the Garden of Eden, and then moving on to the burning bush, the pillar of fire by night and the cloud by day that led the children of Israel through the wilderness, the star of Bethlehem, and other instances in Scripture, the Shekinah glory reappears. Jesus is the ultimate Shekinah glory—the visible presence of God—on earth.

Note how many times the Angel of the Lord appeared in the Old Testament era. Most think this was actually Jesus. He was the uniquely born one—the holy one of Israel—born of a virgin by the Spirit of God.

Jesus fulfilled and gave meaning to every mark and letter of the Mosaic Law. Jesus fulfilled every longing of the heart of the Psalms. And Jesus also fulfilled the many messianic prophecies. These prophecies seem to speak of Jesus and find their culmination in him, so look for those themes that find their way to Jesus.

3. Count on his wisdom. If you are seeking to hear and listen to the voice of Jesus, ask for his wisdom as you live your life the best you can. In one of the early writings of the New Covenant—the book of James—we read: "If any of you lacks wisdom, you should ask God, who gives generously to all without finding fault, and it will be given to you."[209] Take this advice.

I do. I ask for wisdom every day, sometimes many times a day, and I count on it as I make decisions, wanting to hear the voice of Jesus as I move through the day.

4. Be sure to seek Jesus within the context of a few. One of the most important ways for you to hear the voice of Jesus is to operate within a supportive community, learning to hear and practice his words together. Remember, it's when two or three are gathered together in the name of

Jesus that Jesus will show up and make his presence known. When this happens, you will recognize and hear his voice through another.

5. Discipline yourself to listen when you pray. When you pray, don't do all of the talking and asking; take time to listen for an answer. This seems so simple, yet it is difficult to do. It takes discipline to sit quietly and listen.

6. Trust Jesus. When it comes to hearing the voice of Jesus, this may be the most critical dimension of all!

Near the Sea of Galilee, Jesus was asked, "What must we do to do the works God requires?"[210]

Jesus answered this most simply: "The work of God is this: *to believe in the one he has sent.*"[211]

Learn to trust Jesus with your security, your family, your business, your future—everything! When you have the courage to trust Jesus with everything, believe me, you will hear what he has to say. This is the ultimate expression Jesus is looking for as you learn to respond to his most revolutionary words ever: *Follow me!*

When you are overwhelmed with troubles and trials, ask Jesus about it. He's been there, done that. When you can't stand the pain any longer, ask Jesus. He's been there, done that. When you feel betrayed, rejected, and discounted, ask Jesus. He's been there, done that. When you just lost your loved one by death, ask Jesus. He's been there, done that. When God seems to be late coming through for you, ask Jesus about it.

If you want to make Jesus your end game, your best action step is to take whatever is on your mind and heart to Jesus first. When I find myself talking about my problems more to people than I do to Jesus, then I know Jesus isn't my end game.

Jesus Is More...

Today, Jesus of Nazareth stands at the highest pinnacle of all humanity. One clue that this is true: there are over 147 million items in the Library of Congress, extending to over 838 miles of bookshelves, and more of them are about Jesus than any other person who ever lived!

Jesus is a great man, yet he is more than just a great man. His life and lifestyle speak more loudly than his teachings. When it comes to making sense out of life, all you have to do is ask the question "What would Jesus do?" and you already have your answer! This is a universal question that anyone (Christian, Muslim, Jew, Buddhist, Hindu, nonreligious) can ask and be helped by the answer. Jesus' is the only lifestyle that can be said to be the lifestyle of the universe. The lifestyle of the universe is not a code; it's a character. His name is Jesus. Jesus has become a reference point for moral behavior for many.

Jesus is the most quoted teacher ever, yet he is more than a teacher. You would be hard pressed to find any self-help principles taught today that do not find their origin in the teachings of Jesus. His wisdom and insights rank higher than those of any spiritual guru. In fact, several of the most recent self-help gurus used Jesus as their source—without giving him any credit.

Jesus stands alone as a prophet, yet he is more than a prophet. I'm fascinated that one of the best known of the Hindu culture, Mahatma Gandhi, purposely followed the teachings and example of Jesus. Gandhi was so adored by his people that he was called Christlike. I'm amazed that the best-known Buddhist, His Holiness the 14th Dalai Lama, Tenzin Gyatso, said that he is unworthy of tying the shoes of Jesus.

It's well known that the Holy Bible treats Jesus as a great prophet, but few know that the Holy Qur'an presents him as the only supernatural prophet. Even Jewish scholars have begun to recognize Jesus as the most popular rabbi ever. Agnostics and atheists have lots of trouble with religion, but not with Jesus. I know Muslims, Jews, Buddhists, Hindus, Christians, atheists, and agnostics who follow Jesus and view him as more than a prophet. This is the Jesus movement under way.

Jesus is more than a great man, more than a good teacher or guru, more than a credible brand, and more than a prophet. These are proper labels for Jesus and all true. These labels, however, don't necessarily make a difference in a person's life . . . *until* you make Jesus your end game.

Conclusion

Thank you for following me on this journey of words. I hope it encourages you to follow the One who is the way, the truth, and the life.

I can't say the journey will be easy.

I can say you will never regret it.

As a postscript to what I have written, I want to share with you a quote from Albert Schweitzer. But before I get to the quote, let me first say a little about who Schweitzer was.

He had three doctorates—in philosophy, theology, and medicine. He was also a well-respected author. On top of that, he was a concert organist and a world-class authority on Bach. Yet he left his ivory-towered world, with its promises of fame and fortune, and transported himself to Africa for a life of service to the poor and needy.

Why?

Because he was a follower of Jesus. And Africa is where Jesus led him.

Although some of his theological beliefs were unorthodox, his devotion to Jesus was one of unswerving obedience. He read the story of the rich man and Lazarus in the Bible and realized that Europe was the rich man and Africa was Lazarus. He felt compassion for the plight of the people there, and he decided that once he finished his medical degree, he would dedicate the rest of his life to serving them. He touched them and healed them, much the way Jesus did when he walked the earth. He fed them and gathered them together, much the way Jesus did. And he did this for almost sixty years, until the day he died. He was dedicated to serving humanity in the name of Jesus and had a clear understanding of the Kingdom of God.

Here's the quote I mentioned earlier. (I can't stop thinking about it!)

> [Jesus] comes to us as One unknown, without a name, as of old, by the lake-side. He came to those men who knew Him not. He speaks to us the same word: "Follow thou me!" and sets us to the tasks, which He has to fulfill for our time. He commands. And to those who obey Him, whether they be wise or simple. He will reveal Himself in the toils, the conflicts, the sufferings which they shall pass through in His fellowship, and, as an ineffable mystery, they shall learn in their own experience Who He is.[212]

There is a part of Jesus we can't know by reading books about him, can't know by listening to sermons on him. There is a part of him we can't know by going to Church, to Bible college, to seminary. There is a part of him we can only know by following him. The way Peter followed him. And James. And John. And the rest of the original Twelve.

As they walked with him, they watched him and worked with him. He showed them things he never showed to the masses, shared with them things he never shared with the crowds. He answered their questions. He spoke into their lives. He loved them. Taught them. Washed their feet. As Schweitzer said, he revealed himself in the toils, the conflicts, and the sufferings that they passed through in his fellowship. And, again as Schweitzer said, they learned in their own unique experience who Jesus is.

Simply Jesus.

An incredible offer is extended to you with the words "Follow me." Come along with us—won't you?—and follow him.

Come and be challenged.

Come and be changed.

The world will be a better place if you do. *Your* world will be a better place if you do.

About the Author

Tim Timmons is a professional speaker, author, blogger, and mentor to those who are "leaning in." Tim is comfortable and effective as he communicates to men and women who come from the diverse cultures of the world. He and Diana prefer to work as a team to advance the conversation of Jesus around the world. They have five children, fourteen grandchildren, and live in Newport Beach, California.

Notes

1 Columbus was quoting from the Spanish Requirement of 1513 (*El Requerimiento*), a statement from the monarchs asserting Spain's divine right to take possession of the territories of the New World. Spaniards were instructed to read the Requirement to the native people—who did not understand Spanish—to give them an opportunity to submit before being attacked. For a translation of *El Requerimiento*, see http://www.nlm.nih.gov/nativevoices/timeline/178.html.

2 Luke 22:49–51.

3 John 14:5.

4 John 14:6.

5 Matthew 11:28–30 (MSG).

6 Mark 3:13–19.

7 See Luke 9:28–35 (NIV).

8 Matthew 26:34–35.

9 Matthew 26:69–75.

10 See John 21:15.

11 Mark 7:1–13.

12 John 5:39–40 (NIV).

13 Chip Brogden, "Is Jesus Enough?" The School of Christ, http://theschoolofchrist.org/articles/is-jesus-enough.html.

14 Luke 17:20–21.

15 Jag Parvesh Chander, ed., *Teachings of Mahatma Gandhi* (Lahore: Indian Printing Works, 1947).

16 Ibid.

17 Ibid.

18 Ibid.

19 Tenzin Gyatso, "Many Faiths, One Truth," *New York Times*, May 24, 2010, http://www.nytimes.com/2010/05/25/opinion/25gyatso.html?_r=0.

20 David Flusser with R. Steven Notley, *The Sage from Galilee: Rediscovering Jesus' Genius*, 4th ed. (Grand Rapids, MI: Eerdmans, 2007).

21 Albert Einstein, interview by George Sylvester Viereck, "What Life Means to Einstein," *Saturday Evening Post,* October 26, 1929, http://www.saturdayeveningpost.com/wp-content/uploads/satevepost/what_life_means_to_einstein.pdf.

22 Mark D. Siljander, *A Deadly Misunderstanding: A Congressman's Quest to Bridge the Muslim-Christian Divide* (New York: HarperOne, 2008).

23 John 1:46; 4:29.

24 Matthew 16:15 (NIV).

25 Matthew 16:16 (NIV).

26 Matthew 16:17 (NIV).

27 Wayne Martindale, Jerry Root and Linda Washington, *The Soul of C. S. Lewis,* (Tyndale House Publishers, 2010), page 223.

28 Ibid.

29 I don't think they actually knew the things I was sharing, but they nodded with enthusiastic agreement. It was from their Qur'an and they loved it that we loved what we had discovered about Jesus there.

30 See John 4:17–18.

31 See John 4:21–24.

32 John 4:26.

33 John 4:29 (NIV).

34 John 4:39–41.

35 Matthew 15:28 (NIV).

36 Matthew 8:5–10 (NIV).

37 Matthew 8:11–12 (NIV).

38 Matthew 8:13 (NIV).

39 Genesis 12:2–3 (MSG).

40 There is no word for "Gentile" in the Hebrew or the Greek. The words that are normally translated "Gentiles" are actually the words for "nations" or "cultures."

41 Isaiah 56:7 (NIV), emphasis added.

42 Luke 2:30–32 (NIV), emphasis added.

43 Matthew 12:16b–18, 21 (NIV), emphasis added.

44 Luke 4:18–19 (NIV).

45 Luke 4:20–21 (NIV).

46 Luke 4:22 (NIV).

47 Luke 4:24 (NIV).

48 Luke 4:25–26 (NIV); see also 1 Kings 17:7-24.

49 Luke 4:27 (NIV); see also 2 Kings 5.

50 Matthew 28:18–19 (NIV), emphasis added.

51 Ralph Winter, "The Two Structures of God's Redemptive Mission," in *Perspectives on the World Christian Movement*, ed. Ralph D. Winter and Steven C. Hawthorne (Pasadena, CA: William Carey Library, 1999).

52 Acts 1:8 (NIV), emphasis added.

53 Luke 9:47–48 (TNIV).

54 Luke 9:49 (TNIV).

55 Luke 9:50 (TNIV).

56 Luke 9:54 (TNIV).

57 Acts 10:9b–16 (NIV).

58 Acts 10:18–20, 23–29 (NIV).

59 Acts 10:34–35 (NIV), emphasis added.

60 Acts 13:45b–47 (NIV).

61 Isaiah 49:6 (NIV).

62 Acts 13: 49–50 (NIV).

63 See Mark 7:9.

64 Matthew 5:19–20 (NIV).

65 Matthew 15:16–20 (NIV).

66 Matthew 23:27–28 (NIV).

67 Matthew 23:5–12 (TNIV).

68 Luke 24:27 (NIV).

69 Matthew 22:34–40.

70 Matthew 9:9 (NIV).

71 Matthew 9:10–11 (NIV).

72 Matthew 9:12 (NIV).

73 Matthew 9:13 (NIV).

74 Hosea 6:6 (NIV).

75 Mark 7:6–8 (NIV).

76 Mark 7:9, 13 (NIV).

77 Matthew 23:23–24 (NIV).

78 Genesis 3.

79 Exodus 32.

80 Acts 8:1; 9:1–2.

81 Acts 9:15-16 (NASB), emphasis added.

82 Acts 9:20–22.

83 Acts 11:26, 26:28; 1 Peter 4:16.

84 See Acts 9:2; 19:9, 23; 24:5, 14, 22.

85 Luke 9:49-50 (NIV).

86 Matthew 16:18 (NIV).

87 Matthew 16:18; 18:17.

88 Matthew 5:17 (NIV).

89 Don Richardson, *Eternity in Their Hearts: Startling Evidence of Belief in the One True God in Hundreds of Cultures Throughout the World*, 3rd ed. (Ventura, CA: Regal, 2005).

90 See Matthew 9:13.

91 Matthew 11:28–30 (NIV).

92 Matthew 10:12–13.

93 Luke 7:50, 8:48.

94 John 14:27 (NASB).

95 John 16:33 (NASB).

96 John 20:21 (NIV).

97 Luke 2:10.

98 John 15:11 (NASB).

99 John 16:24 (NASB).

100 John 17:13 (NASB).

101 Matthew 22:37 (NASB).

102 Matthew 22:39 (NASB).

103 Matthew 22:40.

104 John 13:34–35 (NASB).

105 Luke 6:27, 32, 35 (NASB).

106 John 15:9–10, 12 (NASB).

107 John 17:22–23, 26 (NASB).

108 See Acts 13:38–39.

109 See Chapter 3.

110 Colossians 1:19–20 (MSG).

111 Colossians 2:9–10 (MSG).

112 John 1:18 (NIV).

113 John 5:39–40 (NIV).

114 John 15:1–5 (NIV).

115 John 16:12–15 (NIV).

116 Matthew 4:17 (NIV).

117 Matthew 10:7 (NIV).

118 Luke 17:20–21 (NIV).

119 Matthew 4:17 (NIV).

120 Matthew 5:20 (NIV).

121 1 Samuel 13:14.

122 Matthew 7:21 (NIV).

123 Matthew 7:22–23 (NIV).

124 Matthew 7:24–27 (NIV).

125 Matthew 18:3 (NIV1984); see also Mark 10:15; Luke 18:17.

126 John 3:3–5, 6 (NIV).

127 Matthew 19:16–19 (TNIV).

128 Matthew 19:20–21 (TNIV). See also Luke 18:18–22.

129 Matthew 19:23 (NIV1984).

130 Matthew 19: 24 (NIV1984).

131 Matthew 19:25 (NIV1984).

132 Matthew 19:26 (NIV1984).

133 Matthew 21:31–32 (NIV1984).

134 Matthew 23:13 (NIV1984).

135 Acts 2:42.

136 Gordon, MacKenzie, *Orbiting the Giant Hairball: The Corporate Fool's Guide to Grace* (Shawnee Mission, KS: OpusPocus, 1996).

137 Matthew 12:24.

138 Matthew 13:10 (TNIV).

139 Matthew 13:10–17 (TNIV).

140 Matthew 13:3–9 (TNIV).

141 Matthew 13:18–23 (TNIV).

142 Matthew 13:20, 19, 38 (NIV).

143 Matthew 13:24–30 (NIV).

144 Matthew 13:31–32 (NIV).

145 Matthew 13:33 (NIV).

146 Matthew 13:44–46 (NIV).

147 Matthew 13:47–50 (NIV).

148 Matthew 13:52 (NIV1984).

149 1 Thessalonians 1:3 (NASB).

150 1 Thessalonians 1:9–10.

151 Matthew 18:20 (NIV).

152 For himself: John 17:1–5. For his early disciples: John 17:6–19. For all followers to come: John 17:20–26.

153 John 19:30.

154 John 17:3–26 (NASB).

155 John 17:8.

156 See James 1:22.

157 Matthew 5:13–16.

158 Matthew 18:20.

159 Matthew 18:20.

160 Acts 1:3.

161 Acts 10:39–43 (NIV), emphasis added.

162 Mark 5:21–43 (NIV).

163 Mark 5:34.

164 Luke 19:1–10 (NIV).

165 Luke 19:8 (NIV).

166 Luke 19:9 (NIV).

167 Acts 1.

168 Acts 2:14–41.

169 Acts 3:1–10.

170 Acts 4, 5, and 7.

171 Acts 9.

172 Acts 10.

173 Matthew 4:19, 8:22, 9:9, 10:38, 16:24, 19:21.

174 Matthew 28:19 (NIV).

175 Luke 14:25–26 (PHILLIPS). Note: Jesus is often quoted as saying that he requires you to "hate" your family and to "hate" yourself. But Jesus spoke in Aramaic, and in that language the wording is clearly not "hate" but to "set aside" all others to make Jesus your highest priority.

176 Luke 14:27 (NIV).

177 Acts 9:15.

178 Luke 14:28–30 (PHILLIPS).

179 Luke 14:31–32 (PHILLIPS).

180 Luke 14:33 (PHILLIPS).

181 Luke 14:33 (NIV).

182 Colossians 3:16 (NASB).

183 Galatians 4:19 (NASB).

184 Colossians 1:27 (NASB).

185 Matthew 6:34 (NIV).

186 Matthew 6:33.

187 Exodus 16.

188 Ecclesiastes 12:13.

189 Ecclesiastes 11:8.

190 2 Corinthians 11:3 (NASB).

191 John 4:35.

192 Matthew 5:14–16 (NIV).

193 John 13:34 (NIV).

194 Matthew 5:43–45.

195 1 Peter 3:8–12, 15 (NIV).

196 Romans 12:20 (NIV).

197 Romans 10:14–16 (MSG).

198 Matthew 25:37–39 (NASB).

199 Matthew 25:40 (NASB).

200 Matthew 25:45 (NIV).

201 John 15:5 (NIV).

202 Philippians 3:8.

203 Matthew 24:5 (NIV1984).

204 John 5:39–40 (NIV), emphasis added.

205 John 21:18–19, 21–22 (NIV), emphasis added.

206 Acts 1:8 (NIV), emphasis added.

207 John 10:14–16 (NIV), emphasis added.

208 Luke 24:44–45 (NIV).

209 James 1:5 (TNIV).

210 John 6:28 (NIV).

211 John 6:29 (NIV), emphasis added.

212 Albert Schweitzer, *The Quest of the Historical Jesus* (Mineola, NY: Dover, 2005), 401.

IF YOU ENJOYED THIS BOOK, WILL YOU CONSIDER
SHARING THE MESSAGE WITH OTHERS?

- Mention the book in a Facebook post, Twitter update, Pinterest pin, or blog post.

- Recommend this book to those in your small group, book club, workplace, and classes.

- Head over to timtimmons.com, "LIKE" the page, and post a comment as to what you enjoyed the most.

- Tweet "I recommend reading #SimplyEnough by @ttimmonssr @timtimmons.com"

- Pick up a copy for someone you know who would be challenged and encouraged by this message.

- Write a review on amazon.com, bn.com, goodreads.com, or cbd.com.

You can subscribe to our

Jesus Plus Nothing Daily @ www.timtimmons.com